Beautiful Handmade
NATURAL
SOAPS

Lavender-Citrus
Tea Bath Bags
For a luxurious, relaxing bath,
simmer your Tea Bag in one
quart of fresh water for
10 mins. Then pour into
your bath and enjoy.

BEAUTIFUL HANDMADE
NATURAL
SOAPS

Practical Ways to Make
Hand-Milled Soap and Bath Essentials

Included—Charming Ways to Wrap, Label, & Present Your Creations as Gifts

BY MARIE BROWNING

Sterling Publishing Co., Inc.
New York

Prolific Impressions
Production Staff:

Editor: Mickey Baskett
Copy: Phyllis Mueller
Graphics: Dianne Miller, Michael Moore
Photography: Skye Mason, Jerry Mucklow
Proofing: Jim Baskett
Styling: Laney McClure

Library of Congress Cataloging-in-Publication Data Available

Published by Sterling Publishing Company, Inc.
387 Park Avenue South, New York, N.Y. 10016
Produced by Prolific Impressions, Inc.
160 South Candler St., Decatur, GA 30030
© 1998 by Prolific Impressions, Inc.
Distributed in Canada by Sterling Publishing
c/o Canadian Manda Group, One Atlantic Avenue, Suite 105
Toronto, Ontario, Canada M6K 3E7
Distributed in Great Britain and Europe by Cassell PLC
Wellington House, 125 Strand, London WC2R 0BB, England
Distributed in Australia by Capricorn Link (Australia) Pty. Ltd.
P.O. Box 6651, Baulkham Hills, Business Centre, NSW 2153 Australia

Acknowledgements

Marie Browning thanks the following for their generous contributions:

Scott
Katelyn
Lena
Jonathan
For their understanding, love, and support

Toni Lander
Moonlit Lathers
2835 Pickford Road
Victoria, British Columbia, Canada
For kindly sharing her Bath Blitz secret

Environmental Technology Inc. (ETI)
South Bay Depot Road
Fields Landing, California, U.S.A.
For microwavable soap bases, soap molds, soap color chips

Plaid Enterprises
1649 International Blvd.
P.O. Box 7600
Norcross, Georgia, U.S.A.
For acrylic paints, plaster molds, decoupage papers, and instant transfers

Silk Road Aromatherapy and Tea Co.
1624 Government Street
Victoria, British Columbia, Canada
For essential oils, base oils, glass droppers, glass bottles, spray misters, and aluminum storage tins

Sunflower Health Foods Ltd.
7060 West Saanich Road
Brentwood Bay, British Columbia, Canada
For dried botanicals, pure vegetable soap, and other natural additives

CONTENTS

INTRODUCTION

This book contains practical, easy-to-follow instructions for creating your own hand-milled soap and other bath products. From the experience, perhaps you will develop a kinship with generations of homemakers who, using recipes handed down for centuries, produced bath and beauty products for their households using simple ingredients, herbs from the garden, and natural fragrances.

I've included secrets for hand milling your own soap from a store bought soap base with added ingredients to make a superior, quality bar. The additions to the basic white soap include fragrant essential oils, herbs, flowers, colorants, and rich oils—to greatly improve the quality and appeal of the soap. Recipes are presented for more than 20 different hand-milled soaps. Only simple equipment is required (most of what you need is probably already in your kitchen), and the ingredients are common and readily available in grocery stores, natural food markets, or easily grown in a home garden.

Also included in this book are recipes for bath oils, bath salts (including the Bath Blitz, a solid fizzing bath salt), bath and massage oils, bubble bath, bath scrub bags, and comfort bags. The recipes have basic guidelines and suggested additives and fragrances, but you can alter them easily to create your own blends. I have included information on the individual ingredients that will aid you greatly when you begin to experiment.

There are also a variety of packaging and labeling ideas and plans for creating unique and attractive gift collections with soaps and bath products that will delight family and friends, children and adults—even the family dog!

Most of the money you pay for commercial bath products covers the costs of advertising, packaging, and promoting the products, not for what's in them. You can make your own bath products at home and package them elegantly for a fraction of the cost of store-bought wares. Another advantage is knowing what's in your homemade products—many store-bought products, including soaps, are not required to list their ingredients.

Enjoy the process of creating your own personal care products and fragrance blends and presenting them in a professional, eye-catching manner. It's another way to say, "I care, so I made it myself." ❏

Marie Browning

WHAT IS SOAP?

Soap is the product of a chemical process called saponification, which occurs when acids in the form of animal or vegetable fats are combined with an alkali (a solution of sodium hydroxide and water, called lye) and produce a mixture of soap and glycerine. Quite simply, it's a slippery substance that produces bubbles.

Soapmaking is an ancient craft. Prehistoric people may have discovered soap when fat and ash met and saponified as they cooked over open pits. A soap manufactory was uncovered in the ruins at Pompeii, and the Greek physician Galen wrote about soap in the second century. It's hard to believe that as recent as the last century, soap had to be labeled as to it's use. Also during this time, soap fell out of popularity as some modest Victorians believed "soap baths" as disgraceful and sinful.

Some of the famous brand name soaps that you buy today are actually not soap at all. Nowhere on the packages does the word "soap" appear, rather the products are labeled "beauty bars" or "deodorant bars." They are synthetic detergents. These "beauty bars" also contain chemical components called "builders" that increase the efficiency of the soap.

This book will teach you how to make your own "natural" soaps. Starting with a soap bar, you can add your own natural ingredients, creating a product superior to a synthetic chemical blend that is commercially available. ❏

AROMATHERAPY

Aromatherapy is rooted in herbal and folk medicine traditions which date back to prehistoric times. Ancient Egyptians, Greeks, Romans, Hebrews, Indians, and Chinese documented the use of fragrances for cosmetic and medicinal purposes. Natural aromatics and perfumes were highly prized by early traders.

Aromatherapy came to North America from Europe. The term "aromatherapy" was first used in 1928 by Rene-Maurice Gattefosse, a French chemist who worked in his family's perfume business and became fascinated with the therapeutic potential of essential oils. Not longer afterward, a French physician, Dr. Jean Valnet, began using essential oils for treating medical and psychiatric disorders. Marguerite Maury, a cosmetologist who studied Valnet's research, applied it to beauty therapy and set up the first aromatherapy clinics in France, Britain, and Switzerland. The recent popularity of aromatherapy has made high quality essential oils, fragrance oils, and unscented base products readily available.

It is certainly no surprise that a relaxing, scented bath can soothe us and renew our spirits. Although no medical claims are made here, essential oils of plants are believed to have pharmacological, physiological, and psychological effects, and specific effects and qualities are attributed to them. Here are some of the characteristics attributed to some flowers and herbs:

- **Relaxing:** lavender, clary sage, camomile, ylang ylang, tangerine, rose, lemon verbena
- **Energizing:** rosemary, peppermint, lemon, lime, jasmine
- **Stimulating and uplifting:** Bergamot, orange, jasmine, rosemary, lemon verbena, mint, sage
- **Antiseptic:** tea tree, eucalyptus, peppermint, lavender
- **Soothing:** sage, eucalyptus, lavender, rosemary, rose
- **Relieves insomnia:** camomile, lavender, orange, ylang ylang
- **Helps headaches:** peppermint, clary sage, grapefruit, lavender, camomile
- **Repels fleas, ticks and other small insects:** lavender, rosemary, citronella, camomile, eucalyptus ❏

MAKING HAND-MILLED SOAP

A basic bar of white soap can be further manufactured and enhanced with fragrances, colors, fillers, and oils that the saponification action would normally affect. This process is called hand milling or French milling. The basic soap is transformed by grating it, remelting it, and mixing in additives to greatly improve the qualities of the soap.

Commercially produced hand-milled soap bars are considered the finest quality of soap available for their silky hardness, fragrance, and excellent emollient characteristics. Produced at home, hand-milled soaps are equally exceptional and can be molded and decorated in many creative ways. Using a store-bought soap as a base to make hand-milled soaps makes it possible to create wonderful soaps in an afternoon, rather than the days it would take if you made your own soap.

Making hand-milled soap using store-bought soap is much like making homemade soup; there is no right or wrong recipe. When you make homemade soup, you buy the vegetables from the store, plus the herbs and spices for flavoring and maybe even the stock. It's called homemade even if you didn't grow the vegetables and herbs or raise the chickens and make the stock! It is the same in soap making. You can produce a fine bar of hand-milled soap with a bar of purchased basic white, unscented soap and additives to make it a superior product and still honestly say, "I made it myself."

The advantages of buying the basic soap rather than producing it yourself are obvious. Producing soap from scratch using lye and home rendered fats is a long process where many mistakes can occur, causing failures and disappointing results. In the recipes presented here, the steps are few and simple, but the results are more than pleasing. The skills needed are as simple as boiling a pot of water and the basic equipment may already be in your kitchen. All measurements are done by volume instead of weight so you are not required to buy an accurate scale and thermometers aren't even needed.

For most of us, soapmaking is a process best left to some-one else. The times when I made my own soap base, I always worried that I would splash the caustic, hot lye solution on myself or that complete saponification would not occur and my soap would be harsh and drying to the skin. I prefer to leave soapmaking to the experts. The next time you're at a country market or craft fair, look for someone selling homemade soap. Perhaps the soapmaker would be willing to make a basic soap with no additives for you to use in your hand-milling recipes.

The soap recipes in this book would, however, work just as well if you decide to make your own soap base. Many excellent books and home kits are available to guide you. For beginners, the best home soapmaking kit is one that contains all the required, pre-measured ingredients, molds, and instructions. ❏

SOAPMAKING TERMS

Abrasives - Substances which, when added to soap, gently scrub the skin. Examples: cut luffa sponge, ground almonds.

Additives - Ingredients added to soap during the hand-milling process. These additions impart special characteristics to the finished bar. Examples: addition of extra oils to create a superfatted soap that adds extra moisturizing qualities and makes the soap richer and milder.

Anti-oxidants - Ingredients that retard the deterioration of the soap by preventing natural ingredients, such as fruit or vegetables, from combining with oxygen and becoming rancid. Example: vitamin E oil.

Antiseptics - Substances that inhibit the growth of bacteria on living tissue and in the product. Example: lavender.

Aromatherapy - The use of aromas and essential oils to affect emotional and physical well-being.

Aromatic - Having a fragrant smell and/or taste.

Astringent - In cosmetic terms, a skin cleansing action that contracts the pores and tissues, making them smoother.

Blenders - Additional scents that are combined with a main scent to enhance and fix the scents into a single blended fragrance. Blenders give harmony and maintain the overall balance of a blended fragrance. Example: in a spicy rose scent, the rose is the main scent and cinnamon and clove are added as blenders.

Detergent - A cleanser in which petroleum distillates take the place of natural fats.

Emollients - Ingredients that moisturize the skin, smooth wrinkles, improve elasticity, and protect. Examples: glycerine, almond oil.

Essential oils - Volatile and fragrant oils produced in various parts of flowers and herbs. High quality essential oils impart the beneficial qualities of plants to your fragrance product. Example: lavender essential oil is both stimulating and invigorating.

Fillers - Ingredients that add bulk or extend a product. Example: vermiculite used in carpet deodorizer as a filler and a fixative to hold the scent.

Fixatives - Ingredients that stabilize volatile oils and prevent them from evaporating too quickly. Example: orris root, a common vegetable fixative.

Fragrance oil - A synthetic oil which reproduces the scent of a natural essential oil. The scents closest to the natural scent are the most successful in fragrance technology, and there are wonderful blended fragrance oils that do not exist in nature. Examples: fragrances such as "rain" and "rainforest."

Hand-milling - Soap made by grating a base soap, remelting with water, adding beneficial ingredients, and remolding to produce a superior quality soap.

Herb - A plant used in medicines, as food, or for fragrance which has a soft stem and which, after flowering, dies or withers to the ground. The American Herb Society's official definition is "any plant that can be used for pleasure, fragrance, or physic."

Hydrating - Maintaining or restoring normal proportion of fluid in the body or skin. Used in cosmetics to keep the skin moist, firm, and young looking. Examples: sweet orange oil, rose oil, camomile.

Irritant - A substance that produces irritation or inflammation of the skin. Examples: natural and synthetic substances.

Main scent - The dominant scent to which other scents are added to create a single blended theme. The best fragrances are the result of artful combinations. A single scent has no staying power and does not make a perfume.

Refrigerant - An ingredient which cools inflammation and eases muscle pains. Example: menthol in mint.

Saponification - The chemical process in which fats or oils are combined with an alkali (lye) to produce soap and glycerine.

Spice - A strongly flavored, aromatic substance usually obtained from the seeds or fruit of tropical plants. With a few exceptions, spices are not grown in home gardens in the northern hemisphere. Examples: cinnamon, cloves.

Stimulant - A substance that temporarily quickens the functional activity of the tissues. Example: using a luffa sponge stimulates the circulation.

Superfatting - Extra oils and fats added to a soap that will not be saponified, creating a soap that is usually richer and milder. Superfatted soaps can be successfully created by adding oils to a hand-milled basic soap.

Volatile - Easily evaporated, such as an essential oil that has been extracted from a plant and no longer has the plant's cell structure to hold the scent. Fixatives stabilize oils and help them last longer. ❏

INGREDIENTS

The ingredients used to make hand-milled soap include base soaps, additives, oils, fragrances, and colorants. They can be found in grocery stores, health food stores, drug stores, and crafts stores and can be ordered from catalogues.

It's important to become familiar with ingredients and their qualities before you start. For example, using instant oatmeal instead of regular oatmeal can result in a soggy mess.

Just because herbs and flowers are natural doesn't mean they are harmless in every situation; many deadly poisons come from plants. The herbs and flowers used in the recipes in this book are ones that are generally considered safe. If you would like to learn more, there are many books available to educate you in the safe use of plant material.

CAUTIONS

Almost any substance, natural or synthetic, can trigger allergy or irritate sensitive skin. Although these reactions are annoying, it is possible to avoid a recurrence by eliminating the offending ingredient. You can perform a simple skin test to make sure you aren't allergic to a particular soap by applying a soap and water lather to the tender area on the inside of your elbow. If you are sensitive to any ingredient, your skin will redden or develop a slight rash.

GUIDELINES FOR USING ESSENTIAL OILS

Essential oils are highly concentrated and potent substances. Follow these guidelines when using them.

- **Do not** take internally.
- Avoid all essential oils, natural herb products, and salt baths during pregnancy.
- Always dilute essential oils in a base oil; they are not perfumes that can be applied directly to your skin. Undiluted, they can be extremely irritating to the skin.
- Keep essential oils out of reach of children.
- Don't store essential oils in plastic containers. Some essential oils can dissolve plastics.
- Keep oils away from varnished or painted surfaces. (Cinnamon oil, for example, can strip paint from furniture.)

GUIDELINES FOR USING BOTANICAL INGREDIENTS

Use herbs and flowers that are clean and free of insecticides, fungicides, and chemicals. The sprays used on plants can irritate your skin. I prefer to use plants I have grown myself, but when this is not possible, I purchase dried botanicals from a natural food store or grocery store, or purchase them fresh and dry them myself. **Don't use** botanicals that have been dried for potpourri or flower arranging for soapmaking. They are not required to be food safe, and may contain harmful dyes or chemicals.

POSSIBLE ALLERGIC REACTIONS

- Cocoa butter, coconut oil, and almonds may produce a reaction in people allergic to chocolate and nuts.
- Natural emollients such as lanolin and glycerine may cause a reaction in people with sensitive skin.
- Honey may cause a reaction in those allergic to pollen.
- Powdered orris root causes an allergic reaction in those sensitive to perfumes.

SAFETY CONCERNS IN SOAPMAKING

- **Always** melt wax in a double boiler. Wax is very flammable and should never be melted over direct heat.
- Be careful when working with melted soap. It can be very hot and can cause burns if spilled. Microwavable soap bases are especially hot when melted. Always have an adult work with children when making soap.
- Spilled soap or oil is slippery and can cause dangerous falls. Clean up spills immediately.
- Clearly label porous tools, such as wooden spoons and plastic molds, used for soapmaking so they won't be used in food preparation. (While not dangerous, you don't want your food to taste like soap or roses!) Glass items are not porous and will not retain scents and residues.
- Clearly label your finished products with the contents and instructions for use. Some of these soaps smell so yummy someone may mistake them for something edible! ❏

START WITH A BASE SOAP

The criteria for selecting a base soap for hand milling are that the soap be white, unscented, and not a detergent. Unscented, hypo-allergenic soaps, such as baby soaps and pure vegetable soaps, are the best performers in hand-milled soap recipes. They may be harder to find in grocery stores, but they are readily available in drug stores and health food stores. When you shop for soap, you'll find detergent bars that are labeled "beauty bars," "deodorant bars," or "family cleansing bars." The word "soap" does not appear anywhere on the package. The recipes in this book don't use deodorant bars or family cleansing bars because they contain fragrances and colors. Beauty bars are available without scent and color, but if you use beauty bars in your soapmaking you are including the additives, such as fillers, builders, and binders, that are present in them. Unscented beauty bars can be used for facial scrubs—they are not remelted, so the moisturizing cream they contain is beneficial. When making hand-milled soaps, best results are obtained with actual soap.

Transparent soaps are also a pleasure to use. Their fragrances are a less expensive way to introduce fragrance blends to melted basic soap. Transparent soaps melt the same as the opaque soaps and produce translucent hand-milled bars. When you start with a transparent soap base, the resulting hand-milled soap is more translucent than transparent. ❏

OILS USED IN SOAP MAKING

Vegetable oils are used as additives in hand-milled soaps to produce superfatted soaps and are used as the base or carrier oil for bath and massage oils. In bath and massage oils, the base oils carry and dilute the concentrated essential oils. They also inhibit evaporation, acting like a fixative, and are quickly absorbed into the skin.

Almond Oil - Almond oil, pressed from the nuts of the almond tree *(Prunus communis),* is the finest and best all-purpose carrier oil. Neutral, unscented, and non-allergenic, it is easily absorbed into the skin where it nourishes and moisturizes. Sweet almond oil, the variety of almond where the familiar nuts are from (var. *dulcis*) is superior, but a great deal more expensive. Buy pure pressed oil that has been extracted without the use of toxic chemicals.

Baby Oil - Baby oil from a pharmacy is a delicate, soothing, very gentle oil that imparts a soft fragrance when used as a base for bath oils. Use it with floral blends.

Castor Oil - Castor oil, from the castor bean plant *(Ricinus communis),* is a pure, natural emollient oil that penetrates the

surface layers of the skin and makes skin softer and more pliable. It is an ideal base for bath oils as it readily disperses in water and will not leave a ring around the bathtub. Castor oil adds richness and mildness to hand-milled soaps and is especially valued for its conditioning qualities in solid shampoo soaps. Used alone in hand-milled recipes, it produces a soft soap. For an odorless, high quality oil look for cold pressed, cold processed castor oil.

Cocoa Butter - Cocoa butter is a fat from the crushed seeds of the cacao tree that is separated during the process of making cocoa. Cocoa butter is solid at room temperature but melts at body temperature, making it a perfect base for a solid massage bar. Look for it at candy making supply stores (it's

continued on next page

Top row, left to right: Olive oil, castor oil, almond oil, baby oil
Bottom row, left to right: Cocoa butter, vitamin E oil capsules, coconut oil, palm oil

OILS USED IN SOAP MAKING

continued from page 13

used in chocolate making) and at drug stores. Cocoa butter improves hand-milled soap by making it creamy and hard. It is also a good emollient and conditioner.

Coconut Oil - Coconut oil, from the coconut palm, is a light textured, odorless white oil that is solid at room temperature but melts readily at 83 degrees F. Coconut oil is absorbed quickly and is an excellent cleanser. It is an excellent addition to hand-milled soaps for its moisturizing and quick lathering qualities. Too much, however, can be drying. Coconut oil is also used in margarines, brake fluid, and baked goods. Look for it at bakery suppliers and Asian markets.

Olive Oil - Olive oil is a healing and soothing bath oil when blended with other base oils. It brings stable lather, emollient qualities, and conditioning to hand-milled soaps and solid shampoo bars. Castile soap is made using olive oil as the main fat. Look for cold pressed, extra-virgin olive oil at grocery and health food stores.

Palm Oil - Palm oil comes from the fruit of a variety of palm tree. It is a white, hard, and brittle oil at room temperature and makes the hand-milled soap it is added to harder with a fluffy lather. It contributes little to skin care.

Safflower Oil and **Sunflower Oil** - Safflower oil (*Carthamus tintorius*) and sunflower oil are inexpensive bases for bath oils that can become rancid more quickly than other base oils. Adding vitamin E oil helps extend shelf life of safflower oil; sunflower oil naturally contains vitamin E and so has a slightly longer shelf life than safflower oil. These oils can be used as fillers when blended with higher quality oils, such as almond, olive, or coconut. They are used extensively in cooking and are readily available at grocery stores.

Vitamin E Oil - Vitamin E oil is an excellent healing oil and an exceptional anti-oxidant in bath oils where botanicals have been added. I use vitamin E oil in hand-milled soap recipes containing fresh fruit or vegetables. Vitamin E oil capsules cost less than liquid Vitamin E oil. To use, cut or pierce the capsule and squeeze out the oil. ❑

FRAGRANCES

Fragrant oils are a significant part of creating bath products. Scents from botanicals and additives are not strong enough for beautiful, aromatic products. Fragrant oils are the most expensive ingredients you will buy, but they are the most important. Do not buy cheap oils or extracts. You will be disappointed.

Essential Oils are the main fragrance oils used. Essential oils are distilled directly from botanicals. They come from flower petals, leaves, wood, spices, roots, fruits, and rinds. Essential oils are more expensive than synthetic fragrance oils, but are superior. Synthetic oils do, however, offer blends and scents that are unobtainable as essential oils. I use both essential oils and synthetic fragrance oils in my beauty product recipes.

Scents are personal. When you purchase fragrance oils, let your nose decide. Many of my blends have a citrus or minty base, as I love those fresh, invigorating aromas. My preference for these scents is reflected in my recipes, and they may not be your personal favorites. (For example, I don't like the earthy aroma of patchouli, but if you like it, use it.)

When buying fragrance oils, carry along a bag of fresh ground coffee to sniff. It helps clear your nose. Otherwise, everything will start to smell the same, and you won't be able to distinguish one fragrance from another.

BASIC FRAGRANCE BLENDING

Fragrance blends have three key elements. The **main scent** is the basic scent in your blend. **Blenders** are additional scents that enhance the main scent. The **fixative** helps give the blend a long-lasting quality and releases the fragrance over time. Fixatives can be unscented or add their own aromas to the blend. The fixative can be the base soap, the base oil, salts, or dried botanicals.

Fragrance oils that combine well with most scents (making them more foolproof for beginners) include lavender, bergamot, rose, vanilla, and cinnamon.

TIPS FOR ADDING FRAGRANCE OILS:

- When adding essential oil to a hand-milled soap recipe, add the oil right before you pour the soap into the mold. If you add the oil too soon, the heat of the soap mixture will evaporate most of the scent.
- Hand-milling requires far less oil for aroma than soap from scratch. You can use drops rather than ounces to scent your soap.
- Some oils are much stronger than others, so the amount of fragrance needed depends on the scent you select. Whatever the scent, make it stronger that you think you need, as some of it will dissipate.

Fragrance Groups

Fragrances are classified by their main characteristic. In this book, I use the term "fragrance oils" to describe oils used for scenting. Choose your scents according to your budget and your nose. * Essential oils are marked with an asterisk.

Citrus Scents
Bergamot*
Sweet orange*
Tangerine*
Lime*
Grapefruit*
Lemon*

Spicy Scents
Clove*
Cinnamon*
Vanilla*

Herbal Scents
Rosemary*
Sage*
Eucalyptus*
Bayberry
Peppermint*

Earthy Scents
Musk
Patchouli*
Amber
Sandalwood*

Floral Scents
Rose*
Jasmine*
Lavender*
Camomile*
Ylang ylang*
Violet*

Fruity Scents
Blackberry
Mango
Coconut

Blended Fragrance Scents
Rain
Ocean
Rainforest
Dewberry ❏

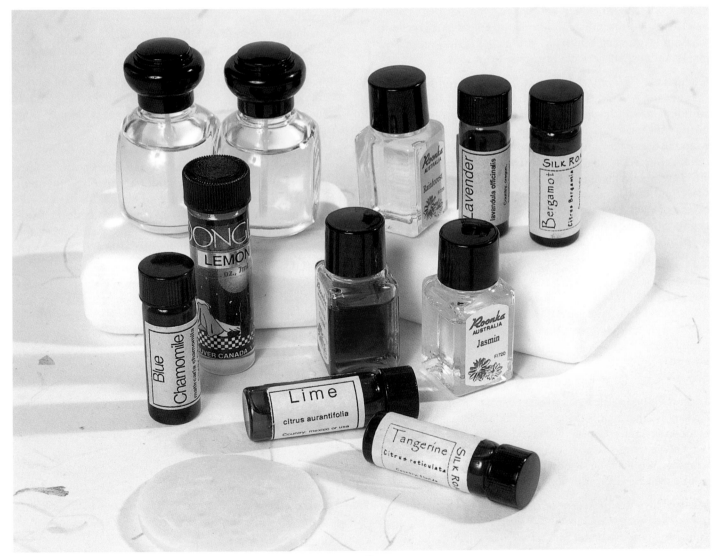

BOTANICAL ADDITIVES

Throughout human history, plants have provided shelter, utensils, fragrance, medicine, and flavor. They have a long tradition as health and beauty aids.

Some of the sweetest scents in the world are those of plants. Not only do they add aroma; most have specific attributes as beauty aids. The listing here is a small sampling of botanicals available to use in your projects. These are easy to find or grow, are effective, and have wonderful perfume. Because some plants are irritants and potentially dangerous, please limit your use of botanicals to these—they are considered generally safe. To learn more, consult botanical journals and reference books for information about useful plants.

Camomile - Both Roman camomile *(Chamaemelum nobile)* and German camomile *(Matricaria recutica)* are fragrant and useful. The name comes from the Greek *Chamaimelon,* meaning "apple on the ground" because the plant has a strong apple scent. Camomile's fragrance is fresh and soothing. Dried camomile, added to bath scrub bags and soap or as a decoration in bath oil, is said to be relaxing, help relieve headaches, aid insomnia, and act as a flea and bug repellent. Camomile grows wild in parks, school yards, and vacant lots almost everywhere and can be grown from seed.

Citrus Peel - Whole, cut, or powdered peels and juice from oranges, limes, lemons, and grapefruit are useful and fragrant additions to your recipes. The fresh scents of citrus are energizing, stimulating, and uplifting. Men's products benefit from the use of lime and sweet orange; children love the scent of tangerine and pink grapefruit. Dried citrus peel is used as a fixative in bath herb blends to enhance and hold the scents. Use fruit that has not been sprayed or dyed. (I prefer organic Seville oranges from the health food store for use in fragrance products.) Air dry peels for use in bath bags. When you wish to use dried orange slices for decoration, use a dehydrator for the best results.

Lavender - Its Latin name, *lavare,* means "to wash." This evergreen plant *(Lavandula angustifolia)* with purple flowers was valued by the ancients for its relaxing and soothing qualities and its antiseptic and healing characteristics. Its bright, strong floral fragrance is the main scent of many perfumes. Lavender can be used in hand-milled soap formulas, as a bath herb, as a flea repellent in pet preparations, and as decoration.

Lemon Verbena - Lemon verbena *(Aloysia triphylla)* has a floral-lemon scent that is delicate and stimulating. Its long, fragrant leaves are a favorite additive in hand-milled soap and bath scrub bags. Lemon verbena is found in health food stores (it also makes a wonderful calming tea). **Lemon balm** can be used in place of lemon verbena in recipes.

Mint - The refreshing scent of mint is a stimulating addition to bath and soap preparations. Of the different types of mints available, some are better for culinary use (such as the mildly scented apple mint) and some are so strong (such as pennyroyal) that only very small amounts should be used. I prefer peppermint *(Mentha piperita)* for its strong, fresh scent. It is high in menthol, which is cooling in beauty preparations, and is an excellent antiseptic. Mints are extremely easy to grow—so easy, in fact, that some gardeners consider them invasive.

Rose - The most popular and irresistible of all the floral scents. Old fashioned tea roses are best for their high oil content of fragrant oil. Look for the word *"damascena"* when choosing highly scented varieties. I also like decorating with the rosebuds from climbing miniature roses. Rose is a good main scent for blending fragrance products. I prefer a slight spicy note in rose blends to fix the scent and make it even more exotic. Use only clean, unsprayed rose petals in your products.

Sage - The name sage is from the Latin *salvere,* meaning to be in good health. Sage has antiseptic, astringent, and healing properties. Its strong scent is relaxing, stimulating, and uplifting. Use its healing qualities to aid problem skins in bath bags and hand-milled soap. It's easy to grow. In addition to the familiar silver-green sages, there are purple- and green-and-gold-leaved varieties.

Scented Geraniums - Scented geraniums *(Pelargonium)* are grown for their fragrant foliage, not for their small pale flowers. There are dozens of scented geraniums; my favorites are rose, lemon, ginger, peppermint, and coconut. (I also grow chocolate mint and pink champagne for fun!) You have to grow your own—I have never seen the dried leaves for sale. The plants are available at garden centers and by mail order. Scented geraniums are beneficial for dry, oily, and problem skins.

GROWING AND GATHERING HERBS AND FLOWERS

Most herbs and many flowers are very easy to grow, either in the garden or in containers. Seeds and small plants can be purchased at garden centers and farmers' markets. Here are some tips for gathering and harvesting your own plants.
continued on next page

Scented Geranium

Peppermint

Lavender

Sage

Lemon Verbena

Camomile

continued from page 16

- Collect the plants in dry weather, at mid-morning when the dew has dried and the sun is not yet high. The aromatic oils are at their greatest strength just before the flowers bloom.

- Hang drying is the simplest way to quickly and successfully dry your plants. Strip off the bottom leaves from the stem, gather the flowers or leafy herbs in a small bundle, and secure with an elastic band. Hang upside down in a dark, dry, well ventilated room on wire hangers away from direct sunlight. The sun will rob the plants of the valuable oils and leave them brittle.

- Air drying is best for multi-petaled flowers such as roses. When you want the whole flower head for decoration, hang the flowers to dry. When you want to use petals only, it's best to remove all the petals from the flower heads and air dry them in a single layer in shallow cardboard boxes. The petals will shrink quite a bit as they dry. Transferring them to baskets will save space as the drying process continues. Never add fresh petals to partially dried petals.

- Learn to properly identify your plants and when you cut them for drying, label them right away. One dried leaf looks very much like any other dried leaf!

- After you have stripped the leaves from dried herb stems, don't throw them away! You can use them to add to the pleasure of a cozy fire with a **Fragrant Fire Bundle**. Group together the dried stems of rosemary, lavender, mint, and sage and tie into a neat bundle with raffia. Toss the bundle on the fire for a pleasant natural scent. ❏

COLORANTS

I prefer to use natural additives to color my hand-milled soaps. The resulting soap has an earthy look and the natural hues are attractive. Many of the soap recipes in this book have no added colorants; their hues are the result of the colors of ingredients, which give a decorative aspect to the finished products.

Though it is sometimes pleasing to add color to soap, bath oils, bubble baths, and bath salts, I try to keep synthetic additions to a minimum. You can quickly tell if too much color has been added to your hand-milled soap—just wet the soap and lather up. If the bubbles are colored and not pure white, too much color was added. Colored soaps are always darker when freshly made and will lighten as they dry. Lighter shades are generally more pleasing.

I don't use natural minerals for coloring. If you decide to use them, research them carefully. Some natural pigments, such as cadmium red, are poisonous.

NATURAL POWDERS

Powdered spices, herbs, and flavorings give your hand-milled soap soft, natural hues. Add them to the mixture when the fragrant oils are added and mix well. The powders will not completely color all the bits of soap, but the resulting soap will be pleasantly speckled. You can find powdered spices, herbs, and flavorings at grocery and health food stores. Here are some suggestions:

Turmeric - Adds a golden orange hue. Use very little to avoid altering the scent of the soap.

Paprika - Adds peachy tone with red specks. Too much will make your soap abrasive.

Dried Calendula Blossoms - Finely grind these dried flowers for a natural ocher to yellow hue. They add texture to your soap.

Cinnamon - Contributes warm brown speckles. Be careful not to add too much or your soap will be scratchy. If you add cinnamon powder at the beginning of melting, your soap will be a warm dark brown color.

Cocoa Powder - Add cocoa powder to a small amount of one of the oils before mixing it in. The result will be a light, warm brown. Cocoa powder is a nice addition to solid massage bars if a very little is used. Adding too much will affect the overall aroma.

CANDLE DYES

Concentrated candle dyes are synthetic compounds that come in small solid blocks of wax. Their strong colors give a pleasant, decorative look to bath oils. These colorfast dyes are found at crafts stores.

To use candle dye in bath oil and hand-milled soap recipes follow these steps:

1. Place 2 tablespoons safflower or sunflower oil in a glass measuring cup.
2. Slice off a few slivers of the candle wax and add to the oil. When creating your own hues, always start with the lightest color and add other, darker colors in small amounts until the desired shade is achieved.
3. Heat the oil in the microwave or in a water bath until the dye melts. Stir to help the dye disperse. When the desired shade is reached, add to soap at the time the fragrant oils are added. For bath oils, add the dye mixture slowly and mix in well. Keep adding color until the desired shade is reached.

SOAP DYES

These are available where soap making supplies are sold. Soap dye is concentrated dye already incorporated into base soap. Grate and add to melted soap.

FOOD COLORING

Food coloring can be used to color bath salts and bubble bath—not in hand-milled soap. For coloring bubble bath, add a few drops when blending the ingredients. For coloring bath salts, add a few drops to 2 tablespoons of the salts used in the recipe. Stir to evenly distribute the color, then mix with rest of the salts in the batch.

To make layered bath salts, divide your salt mixture and color it a variety of hues. Spoon different colors of salts into a clear container for a decorative, layered look. You can scent each color with a different fragrance to create fun fragrance blends.

Food coloring is not suitable for hand-milled soap recipes because the color fades, and it's not suitable for bath oils as the dyes are not oil-soluble.

Pictured at right:
Top row, left to right: Red food coloring, blue candle dye, blue food coloring, yellow food coloring
Middle row, left to right: Cinnamon, yellow soap dye, green soap dye
Bottom row, left to right: Paprika, turmeric, violet candle dye

OTHER INGREDIENTS

Other ingredients used for creating fragrant bath products include natural additives, salts, and fillers. They can be found at grocery stores, health food stores, and crafts stores and ordered from herb suppliers.

Almonds - Ground, blanched almonds are added to hand-milled soap and facial scrubs for their cleansing, slight bleaching action, and gentle abrasive qualities. The ground almonds also add a pleasant nutty fragrance.

Banana - This tropical fruit is added to soap for its light scent and soft texture.

Beeswax - A highly fragrant natural animal wax from the comb of the honey bee. It has a golden amber color and a sweet honey fragrance. It is valued in cosmetics for emulsifying creams and ointments. For hand-milled soap recipes, add the melted wax near the beginning of the melting process and stir well. If the wax cools in the soap before blending you will end up with hard bits in your soap. Beeswax makes your bars softer to the touch with a slight honey scent. **CAUTION:** Always melt beeswax in a double boiler. It is highly flammable.

Cinnamon - Powdered cinnamon added to hand-milled soap will add both a warm spicy scent and a soft speckled brown coloring. Using too much will make the soap scratchy. It also works as an astringent and a stimulant in bath products. Cinnamon sticks are used to decorate packaging.

Coffee - Coffee, when used in soaps, absorbs odors from the skin. Use fresh, unbrewed ground coffee. This makes a great kitchen soap bar to remove food smells from hands after food preparation.

Cornmeal - Cornmeal can be added to hand-milled soaps as a gentle abrasive. It is also used in bath scrub bags instead of oatmeal for those with oily skin.

Distilled Water - For my soap making, I use tap water. Where I live, the water is of excellent quality and very soft. If you live in an area that has hard water (soap doesn't lather well), you may wish to use bottled distilled water in your hand-milled soap.

Dishwashing Soap or Detergent - This is your base for making bubble bath. (Remember, most "soaps" we use are detergents.) I like mild, clear formulas with added vitamin E. Clear detergents contain no dyes or harsh irritants. Look for bulk sales at superstores for the best deals.

Flax Seeds - Flax seeds are used to make comfort bags and eye pillows because they hold heat and cold for long periods of time, and the fine, slippery seeds fill out the bags and make them comfortable against your skin. To heat a comfort bag, place in a microwave for 1-1/2 minutes on high. For a cooling bag, store in a plastic bag in the freezer. **CAUTION:** Don't use flax seeds as an additive in hand-milled soaps. They have sharp ends that can irritate and scratch your skin. Only use them encased in a cotton or satin pouch.

Ginger - Ground ginger can be added to soaps to warm the skin. Use it sparingly.

Glycerine - Glycerine, a compound of carbon, hydrogen, and oxygen, is a product of the saponification process. It is a clear, colorless, oily, sticky liquid. Glycerine, widely used in the cosmetic industry as an emollient and humectant, can be added back into soap during the hand-milling process. In bubble bath formulas, glycerine gives the bubbles elasticity and lasting power.

Honey - Honey is produced by bees from the nectar gathered from flowers. Its main components are water and sugar, but there are also small amounts of organic products, such as essential oils from flowers. It is these trace elements that are thought to give honey its curative properties. Honey is an excellent emollient and a nice addition to hand-milled soaps. Adding too much honey will make soap too soft. Adding melted beeswax and honey makes a lovely honey-scented soap. A few drops of citronella oil enhance and strengthen the honey fragrance.

Luffa sponge - *Luffa cylindrica* is a gourd that looks like a fat cucumber. The ripe fruit is soaked, beaten to remove the seeds, and dried. The fibrous skeleton that is left makes a wonderful bath sponge suitable for even the most tender skins. Scrubbing the skin with a luffa improves circulation. A piece of a luffa can be used as a mold—the soap is poured right in it for a unique, all-in-one soap/sponge. Finely cut pieces of luffa can also be added to hand-milled soaps for a gentle, built-in abrasive. Do not put luffa in your food processor or coffee grinder to cut it—it will only stick to the blades and bind up your machine. Place pieces in a bowl and cut the fibers with a pair of sharp kitchen shears.

Oatmeal - Oatmeal gently softens sensitive or irritated skin. It is an excellent bulk material for soothing facial and bath scrub bags. When adding oatmeal to hand-milled soaps, first toast it and grind to a fine powder. Use only regular or long-cooking—not instant—oats.

Powdered orris root - Orris root is the dried rhizome of the iris plant. Historically, it was used as a vegetable fixative for cosmetic products but is no longer used commercially because many people are allergic to it. It is excellent for holding scent in sachets and potpourri blends. Use the powdered form in the Silk Bath recipe as a fixative and to add a slight violet scent.

Petroleum Jelly - Petroleum jelly is a fatty, translucent substance that is a by-product of the petroleum industry. It is widely used in cosmetics as an emollient and barrier cream. Rub it on molds before pouring in the hand-milled soap mixture—when the soap hardens in the mold it will be easy to remove.

Powdered Skim Milk - Milk is a natural cleanser and an excellent additive for hand-milled soaps. I mix powdered milk with honey or oils before adding it to the melted soap to better incorporate it into

continued on next page

continued from page 20

the mix. Powdered milk will soften the soap slightly, so do not use too much. I use instant powdered milk as the base for a luxurious bath. It softens the water and makes your skin feel silky and smooth.

Rose Water - Rose water, a solution of pure essential rose oil and distilled water, is a soothing, emollient liquid with a gentle rose fragrance. Use it instead of water in hand-milled soap recipes for added scent and softening properties.

Vermiculite - Vermiculite is a conditioner sold at garden centers to improve the moisture retaining properties of soil. It is an excellent fixative and filler for carpet deodorizers and fragrant sachet blends. Vermiculite soaks up fragrance oils, taking the place of plant cells for volatile essential oils.

Pictured below:

1. Glycerine	2. Rose water	3. Honey
4. Cornmeal	5. Oatmeal	6. Powdered skim milk
7. Coffee	8. Powdered orris root	9. Flax seeds
10. Banana	11. Luffa	12. Beeswax
13. Cinnamon	14. Ginger	15. Almonds

EQUIPMENT

Most of the equipment you need for making hand-milled soap is probably already in your kitchen. The measurements for the recipes in this book are by volume not by weight, so you use measuring cups and spoons, not a scale.

Glass mixing bowls - Large glass bowls are useful for blending bath salts, holding grated soaps, and blending dried botanicals for scrub bags. When using glass, no fragrance transfer will occur, so the bowls are also safe to use for cooking.

Heat resistant glass measuring bowls - A 4-cup or 8-cup measuring bowl placed in a saucepan of hot water makes an excellent double boiler for melting grated soap, beeswax, and oil/candle dye mixes—the spout on the bowl makes pouring easy. It is also useful for blending bath oils, then pouring them into decorative bottles.

Small heat resistant measuring bowls are also handy for placing measured ingredients into in preparation for soapmaking. These small bowls can be used as containers for melting soap dyes before adding them to the soap mixture.

Large saucepan - A large saucepan (any metal is fine) for heating water to use with a glass measuring bowl as a double boiler.

Glass measuring cups - 1 cup and 2 cup glass measuring cups are needed for measuring grated soap, additives, salts, and other ingredients.

Measuring spoons - A set of metal measuring spoons is needed for measuring smaller amounts of ingredients.

Glass droppers - You will need 2 or 3 glass eye droppers for measuring out your fragrant oils. **Do not** use plastic droppers; some essential oils will dissolve plastic.

Hand Grater - A simple, inexpensive kitchen grater is used for grating soaps for hand-milling.

Food Processor - *(Optional)* A food processor can further process your grated soap, making a smoother, quicker melting soap. Soft beauty bars with moisturizing creams benefit from a quick trip in the processor to make them finer.

Electric spice and coffee grinder - A small grinder is useful for grinding small amounts of additives such as almonds or oatmeal. Clean it after each use by grinding a piece of fresh bread or some rice. The bread or rice soaks up oils and the grinder is easily wiped out with a paper towel.

Wooden spoons - Long-handled wooden spoons are needed to mix melting soap, bubble baths, bath salts, and other blends. Clearly mark the spoons with a permanent pen so you won't use them for cooking.

Drying rack - A wooden or metal rack is useful for drying and curing your soaps. The rack provides air circulation and prevents the soap from warping.

Sharp knife - A sharp knife is needed to slice finished molded soap.

Small plastic funnel - A small plastic funnel is useful for bottling liquid bath products. It keeps the liquid away from neck of the bottle, making a more secure fit for your cork. Use it also for filling comfort bags and masks. ❑

Molds

Molds are required for hand-milled soap, solid fizzing bath salts, and solid massage bars. Molds help make hand-milled soaps look professional and fancy.

Soap molds are available in traditional soap shapes and fun theme shapes. Many molds available are not soap molds at all—these include molds for candy, plaster, and candles and many found objects.

Suggested Molds for Soaps

- **Plastic food storage containers.** A small sandwich or 4" x 6" storage container will accommodate the recipes. Try to find ones with no design on the inside bottom and nice rounded corners.

- **Plastic plaster crafting molds.** There is a wide variety of fun shapes and sizes available to make creative theme soaps. The deep molds work well for solid bath salts. They are available at crafts stores.

- **Flexible red rubber molds.** Flexible molds, made from red rubber are usually used in three-dimensional plaster molding. It is also possible to buy a rubber molding compound for making your own molds from objects. **CAUTION:** Some red rubber molds transfer the color to the soap.

- **Plastic candy molds.** Some candy molds warp, so be careful when using them. Do not use candy molds with microwavable soap bases as the temperatures are too high. Find the molds at shops that sell candy making supplies and kitchenware and at crafts stores.

- **Plastic candle molds.** A wide variety of candle molds is available, including three dimensional molds, pyramid molds, square molds, and molds for wax ornaments. Candle molds are designed to take the high temperatures of melted wax, so they stand up to hot soap without melting.

- **PVC (polyvinyl chloride) pipe.** This is my favorite mold. PVC pipe makes beautiful rounds of soap that fit nicely in the palm of your hand. Pipe is inexpensive, easy to use, and available in a variety of sizes. (I used pipes that were 2", 2-1/2", and 3" in diameter.) Use a hack saw to cut 6-7" lengths; longer ones are harder to handle. Sand all the cut edges smooth and treat insides well with petroleum jelly before each use. To seal the bottom of the mold so the soap doesn't run out, use three or four layers of plastic wrap held on snugly with strong rubber bands. To unmold the soap, remove the plastic wrap from the bottom and push out the soap using a bottle that is slightly smaller than the diameter of the pipe.

- **Soap molds.** Soap molds usually came in kits with microwavable soap bases. Because they are designed for soap, they are the best for molding fancy shapes and stand up to high heat. Avoid very detailed molds when making hand-milled soap from purchased bars. The soap pieces don't dissolve completely, and the soap is too thick and lumpy to fill all the details. Crafts stores carry a nice selection of soap molds.

Mold Release

I found petroleum jelly works well as a mold release. Rub the mold with a thin film of the jelly to ensure easy removal of your hardened soap. I have never had a problem with the soap sticking to the mold or the petroleum jelly making a sticky residue on the soap.

Molds to Avoid

Avoid using hard, inflexible molds made of aluminum or glass, because it is more difficult, but not impossible, to remove the hardened soap from them. If you use them, condition well with a mold release and place in the freezer until solid before attempting to remove the soap.

Because molds must be able to withstand high temperatures of hot, melted soap, avoid plastic cups and disposable plastic containers. The plastic can warp and melt when hot soap is added. Soap shrinks as it cures and dries. Do not use a mold that's too small or shallow—the resulting tiny bar will slip out of your hand and down the drain. ❏

How to Make Hand-Milled Soap

These are general step by step instructions. Specific information on adding scents, colorants, and other ingredients is provided in individual soap recipes. If you aren't following a recipe exactly, remember to note the ingredients used and amounts used as you work. You might produce a bar that you will want to recreate. *In the step-by-step photos we are making the Luffa Scrub Soap.*

Step One
PREPARATION

Gather all the ingredients and measure all the additives. It is important to have all the ingredients ready so you don't have to leave the soap unattended on the stove or prepare the ingredients as the soap is cooling. If you do, you may find your soap has hardened before you get it in the mold.

Measure 1 tbsp. palm oil and place in a container so it is ready to use.

Measure fragrance with a dropper and place it into a glass container so that it is ready to add to melted soap mixture.

All ingredients have been pre-measured and ready to add to melted soap mixture.

PREPARE COLORANTS

Prepare colorants, if you are adding them. Place some oil in a small glass bowl. Shave a few pieces of candle or soap dye into oil. Heat in microwave to melt. Time at 30 seconds, mix then add more time until melted. Mix well. Set aside.

PREPARE MOLDS

Prepare molds by rubbing a thin layer of petroleum jelly on the insides.

If you are using a PVC pipe mold, cover the bottom opening with several layers of plastic wrap and secure with strong rubber bands.

Step Two
GRATE THE SOAP

Grate the soap into a bowl, using a hand grater. For most recipes, you'll grate two to three bars of purchased soap. For a finer textured soap, further process the grated soap in a food processor.

Step Three
MEASURE AND ADD WATER, SOAP, AND OIL

Place the measured grated soap (amounts are specified in individual recipes) in a heat-resistant glass measuring bowl. Add any oil the recipe calls for at this time.

Add water that is called for in recipe.

28

Step Four
PLACE ON HEAT

Place the heat-resistant glass bowl in a saucepan. Add about 2" of water to the saucepan. Place on the stove and turn the burner to medium high. When the water begins to boil, turn heat down, using only enough heat to keep the water simmering. Periodically mix the soap gently as it melts.

THE STAGES OF MELTING

First Stage

The soap will clump together. Use a wooden spoon to break up the clumps and incorporate the water into the soap. Continue mixing. Be gentle so you don't cause too many suds.

continued on next page

Step Four
THE STAGES OF MELTING

Second Stage

As the soap continues to melt, the mixture will become smoother and look like watery cottage cheese. Continue to stir the soap over the boiling water.

Third Stage

In the final stage, the soap looks and acts like lumpy marshmallow cream. It is stringy (this stage is called the "string" or "rope" stage), and all the water has combined with the soap. The mixture quickly becomes thick. It takes 10-15 minutes to reach the final stage. Do not worry if it takes a little longer. You **must** reach the stringy stage before proceeding.

You are now ready to take the glass mixing bowl out of the saucepan of water and add the additional ingredients.

Step Five
ADD COLORANTS

Working quickly, add the colorants, if you are using any.

Step Six
ADD FRAGRANCE

Add the fragrance, if any, now.

Step Six
ADD BOTANICALS AND ADDITIONAL OILS

Add prepared botanicals (herbs, spice powders, flowers, etc.) and additional oils as called for in individual soap recipes.

Step Seven
MIX

Stir the mixture thoroughly to disperse the ingredients.

Step Eight
SPOON INTO MOLD

Spoon the soap mixture into the mold. Tap gently to remove any air bubbles. Let the soap harden.

Step Nine
REMOVE SOAP FROM MOLD

The soap should be hard enough to unmold after four to five hours.

If a soap will not release from the mold, place the mold in the freezer until chilled, and then try to release. (If you are impatient to see your handmade soap, you can harden it quicker by freezing it. Pop it into the freezer until frozen solid, and then unmold.)

Soap also can be hard to unmold if it was not heated long enough to reach the string or rope stage. The soap will not harden and stays soft in the mold. If this happens, just scoop it out and heat the same soap again, allowing it to reheat until it reaches the stringy stage.

You can also salvage a batch that doesn't harden by hand molding the soap into soap balls. See "Hand Molding," page 35.

Step Ten
SLICE

After unmolding, slice the soap into rounds or smaller pieces with a knife. Use a cardboard template to cut the soap to the size and shape you wish. A template also aids in cutting even, straight bars.

Step Eleven
LET DRY ON RACK

Let the unmolded soap dry on a rack and cure for up to three weeks. Turn the soap to prevent warping. Turning the soap is especially important during the first few days.

HAND MOLDING

You can make hand molded soap from any of the soap recipes. Hand molding works especially well for softer soaps.

Here's How:

After the soap has cooled and thickened, scoop out a small handful of the soap and roll into a neat ball. Repeat until all the soap has been molded. Let dry. As the soap cures, press to form firmer, smoother balls. ❏

35

HAND-MILLED SOAP RECIPES

These soap recipes are intended to be used with the step-by-step general instructions for "How to Make Hand-Milled Soap." The soap batches are rather small, using two to three bars of purchased soap to make five or six smaller bars of hand-milled soap. You may want to increase the size of the batches a little, but don't make them too big—larger batches are more difficult. Let your personal taste tell you if you wish more or less of a scent and or a colorant in your batch of soap. The amounts given are suggestions only. ❏

CAMOMILE OATMEAL SOAP

Oatmeal is a popular skin-cleanser, and with the addition of soothing camomile it becomes a mild and gentle face soap. Clary sage adds to the soap's relaxing and healing properties. This recipe makes four 1" thick round soaps in a 2-1/2" diameter or 2" diameter PVC pipe mold.

SOAP RECIPE

Melt together:
2 cups grated soap (an unscented beauty bar can be used)
1/4 cup palm oil
1/2 cup water

Add after the soap has melted:
1 tablespoon ground dried camomile
1 tablespoon ground toasted oatmeal
10 drops camomile oil
5 drops clary sage oil
Optional: a few drops ylang ylang oil, for a more floral scent

Mix the scents and the additives into the soap and pour into the prepared mold. ❏

LUFFA SCRUB SOAP

This simple soap has the gentle scrubbing action of luffa, which gives it an interesting textured appearance. It's up to you to choose the fragrance and decide whether or not to add coloring. This recipe makes four to five 1" slices using a 2-1/2" PVC pipe mold.

SOAP RECIPE

Melt together:
2 cups grated and processed soap
1/2 cup water
1 tablespoon palm oil

Add after the soap has melted:
1 tablespoon finely cut luffa sponge
Optional: A few slivers of violet (or other color) candle dye melted with 1 tablespoon almond oil
18 drops fragrance oil (your choice)

Mix the additives with the melted soap. Pour in the prepared mold. When hardened, push out to unmold and slice into round bars. Cure the soap on a rack, turning often, for about three weeks. ❏

PEPPERMINT REFRESHMENT SOAP

This soap has an invigorating, refreshing scent that lifts your spirits. Peppermint Refreshment soap is a terrific "good morning, let's-get-going" soap. It is molded in a plastic food container. No coloring is used—the peppermint leaves add an interesting spotted appearance. (If you wish to add color, a bright blue-green would be a good choice.) You also can mold this soap in a luffa sponge. (See page 54.) This recipe makes four large rectangular bars or four luffa sponge-soaps.

SOAP RECIPE

Melt together:
2 cups grated soap (an unscented beauty bar can be used for this recipe)
1/4 cup coconut oil
1/2 cup water

Add after soap is melted:
1 teaspoon crushed dried peppermint leaves
10 drops peppermint oil
5 drops rosemary oil
5 drops eucalyptus oil
5 drops tea tree oil

Mix in the fragrance oils and peppermint leaves. Pour the soap into the prepared molds. ❑

MANGO MINT SHAMPOO BAR

This superfatted oil-rich soap rivals expensive salon shampoos. The oils add conditioning qualities without being greasy. The soap is a little soft, and the extra oils inhibit large, fluffy suds, but these are small tradeoffs for beautiful, silky hair.

To use this soap, work up a lather in your hands, then work the lather into your scalp and hair. I cut these bars in a long shape that fits in the palm of your hand for faster lathering. The recipe makes four long, shaped bars.

You can also use this recipe to make a mango mint soap by reducing the amounts of olive oil and castor oil—make both and wrap together for a tropical-themed gift.

SOAP RECIPE

Melt together:
1 cup grated soap
1/2 cup water

Add after the soap has melted:
1/4 cup olive oil
1/4 cup castor oil
1 teaspoon dried crushed peppermint leaves
15 drops mango fragrance oil

Mix the oils and other ingredients well with the melted soap. Pour into a prepared plastic container mold. ❏

Cinnamon Orange Soap

This fresh, energizing soap is a good choice for a man's gift. The palm oil makes the bar hard and long lasting, and the almond oil makes this a superfatted emollient soap. If you wish, add powdered cinnamon to make an attractive speckled bar.

Use a plastic container as a mold. This recipe makes four large bars. I trimmed the edges to make an interesting shape.

SOAP RECIPE

Melt together:
2 cups grated pure vegetable soap
1/2 cup water
1/4 cup palm oil

Add after the soap has melted:
1/4 cup almond oil
10 drops sweet orange oil
5 drops cinnamon oil
Optional: 1/4 teaspoon powdered cinnamon

Mix the fragrance oils and the extra oil into the melted soap. Pour into the prepared mold. ❏

BANANA SLICE SOAP

This yummy smelling soap looked so creamy and luscious that my kids thought I was baking a banana cream pie! The nutrients in the banana enhance the soap's soothing qualities. Vitamin E oil and citric acid act as preservatives to keep the soap fresh. The banana makes the bar soft, so palm oil is added for hardness. If you like, add coconut fragrance oil. It blends with the banana scent for a marvelous tropical aroma. (Use less if you find the scent too strong.) Additional color is optional.

The recipe makes four to five 1" thick slices in a 2" diameter PVC pipe mold. This soap can be gift packaged uncut, allowing the recipient to slice off bars as they are needed.

SOAP RECIPE

Melt together:
2 cups grated soap (unscented beauty bars with added moisturizing cream work well in this recipe)
1/4 cup palm oil
1/2 cup water

Add after the soap has melted:
1/4 of a large, ripe banana with no bruises
1 teaspoon vitamin E oil (about 6-7 capsules)
1 teaspoon citric acid
Optional: 10 drops coconut fragrance oil, a sliver of yellow candle dye melted in 1 tablespoon almond oil

Mash the banana well with the vitamin E oil and citric acid before mixing into the soap. When well mixed, pour into the prepared mold. ❏

AMBER SOAP

A boy or girl with an interest in dinosaurs would love to wash with this soap. Amber is the fossilized resin of coniferous trees that lived over 70 million years ago. Sometimes insects got caught in the resin and were fossilized, too. This soap is a recreation of this natural marvel, complete with a surprise (plastic) bug inside! If you cannot locate amber scented oil, use an earthy perfume like musk or sandalwood fragrance oil.

The soap is molded in two parts so the bug can be placed in the middle. I used a large round mold that accommodated the large plastic bugs I found, but any mold that's deep enough could be used if the bug will fit. Be careful not to add too much dye. You want to be able to see through the soap.

SOAP RECIPE

You'll need:
1 cup microwavable transparent soap base, melted 1/2 cup at a time
A few slivers of soap color dye (to make amber, use yellow plus a bit of red and a bit of black) OR yellow, red, and black candle dye
1 tablespoon grated transparent soap (I used red and yellow shavings)
10 drops amber fragrance oil; 1 plastic bug per mold

First molding:
Melt 1/2 cup of the transparent soap and add the soap color. Stir until the color has melted. (*If using candle dye, melt the slivers of dye in a small amount of transparent soap base.*) Add the fragrance oil and mix well. Pour into the prepared molds, filling the mold only 1/2 full. Let the soaps harden a bit (about 10 minutes). Place the plastic bug on top of this first layer, right side down.

Second molding:
Melt the remaining 1/2 cup of soap base. Before pouring into the mold, stir in the grated colored transparent soap. The colored bits add extra interest (they look like the cracks in real amber). Don't worry if you have small bubbles in this soap - it adds to the effect. ❏

MILK AND HONEY SOAP

Inspired by the Egyptian Queen Nefertiti, who reportedly bathed in milk, honey, and flower pollen, this soft face soap is cleansing and nourishing to make your skin smooth and pliable. The jasmine oil blends with the honey aroma for a soothing and enlivening scent.

Process the grated soap in a food processor for better molding. The additional water in the recipe makes it easier to pour the soap into the mold. This soap needs no added color.

This recipe fills one pyramid mold (I used a candle mold) or makes four smaller flat triangular bars. If you can't find a pyramid mold, pour the soap about 1" thick in a square mold and cut into triangular shapes.

SOAP RECIPE

Melt together:
1 cup grated and processed pure vegetable soap
2/3 cup water

Add after the soap has melted:
1 tablespoon powdered skim milk
1 tablespoon honey
1 tablespoon almond oil
20 drops jasmine oil

Mix the powdered milk, honey, almond oil, and jasmine oil before adding to the melted soap. Mix the additives with the soap and pour into the prepared mold. When hardened, remove from mold and place on a rack to cure. If the soap shrinks a lot and warps, the soap was not heated enough for the excess water to evaporate. ❑

HONEY AND ALMOND SOAP

This soap is just the thing a gardener needs for cleaning up after a day working in the soil. The ground almonds offer gentle abrasive and bleaching qualities. The honey almond aroma is light and soothing, and the honeycomb shape is unique and fun. The almonds, honey, and beeswax give the soap a light scent. If you wish a stronger scented soap, add a few drops each of almond oil and citronella oil.

This recipe makes three to four honeycomb shaped soaps using a 2-1/2" diameter PVC pipe mold.

SOAP RECIPE

Melt together:
1 cup grated and processed pure vegetable soap
1/3 cup water
Add when the soap is melted, but still over the heat:
1 tablespoon melted beeswax
Add after the soap has melted and the beeswax is mixed in:
1 tablespoon honey
1 tablespoon ground almonds
Optional: Small sliver of orange candle dye melted in
1/2 tablespoon almond oil

Mix the additives with the melted soap and pour into the prepared mold. When hardened, push out soap to unmold. Cut in 1" slices. Cut a hexagonal-shaped template (the shape of a section of honeycomb) from thin cardboard. Use the template to cut the shapes. Let the soap cure on a rack, turning often, for three weeks before packaging. ❏

LAVENDER CITRUS SOAP

These old-fashioned soaps are fragrant and stimulating to the skin. This soap will discolor if the lavender buds are added too soon to the melted soap. If you do not like the rough surface and the darkened color, omit the lavender buds and add extra lavender oil. Or, after a week of curing, you can slice thin shavings from the soap to smooth it and remove any dark patches.

SOAP RECIPE

Melt together:
2 cups grated soap
1/2 cup water

Add after the soap has melted:
Oil from 6 vitamin E capsules
1 tablespoon ground dried lemon verbena leaves
1 tablespoon dried lavender buds
10 drops lavender oil
20 drops sweet orange oil

After the soap has cooled and thickened, scoop out a small handful of the soap and roll into a ball. Flatten the ball to create a disk shape. As the soap cures, press the soap into a firmer and smoother shape. If you like, mix a little orange oil with almond oil on your hands and polish the soap smooth. ❏

CITRUS SLICE SOAP

This soap is created with microwavable transparent and opaque soap bases. It is a little more work as it has to be molded twice, but it's well worth the effort to produce these fun and unusual soaps. A pink transparent base would make pleasing pink grapefruit slices.

Two different sized PVC pipe molds (2" diameter and 3" diameter) are needed to create this soap. I prefer to have too much soap rather than too little, so you may want to prepare another mold just in case you have excess melted soap.

The hardest part of making this soap is waiting for it to cool down so you can slice it. It's fun to watch the citrus slices appear!

SOAP RECIPE

First molding:
1-1/2 cups transparent soap base
Soap color dye, color to match the scent
15 drops lime, lemon, tangerine, sweet orange, or grapefruit fragrance oil

Melt the transparent soap base in the microwave or in a double boiler on the stove, adding shaved soap until you get approximately 1-1/2 cups. Add the fragrance oil, mix, and pour into the 2" diameter PVC pipe mold. Let harden and unmold.

Cut the soap:
Cut the soap lengthwise to form the sections of the fruit. First cut the soap in half. Then cut each half into thirds. You will now have six long sections. Do not mix up the sections.

Arrange in the mold:
Place four layers of 8" x 8" plastic wrap on the counter. Arrange the cut soap sections in the center of the plastic. Keep the sections spaced a bit apart so the second pouring of soap will fill the spaces. (Don't be too fussy with the section placement—this is a whimsical soap, and if the pieces are a bit askew it only adds to the charm.) Place the 3" PVC pipe mold over the sections, positioning it so that there is a small space between the mold and the outer edge of the sections. Carefully bring the plastic wrap up around the outside of the mold and secure with rubber bands. Make the plastic as tight as possible around the bottom of the mold.

Second molding:
3/4 to 1 cup melted opaque white soap base
Optional: Soap coloring (Leave this portion white or add a little of the same color used for the transparent sections.)

Melt the opaque soap base in the microwave or in a double boiler on the stove. Carefully pour the melted soap around the transparent sections in the prepared mold. (You may get a little leakage at the bottom if the plastic wrap isn't tight.) Do not move the mold until the soap has hardened. When it is completely cool and hard, push the soap out of the mold. Trim off the top of the soap if bubbles formed. Cut the soap into slices 1" thick. ❏

STRAWBERRY ROSE SOAP

This pretty--although not very practical--soap has a fruity floral scent and is imbedded with small red rose buds. The rosebuds tend to be a little scratchy, and the soap loses the rosebuds quickly with use, but it is a pretty display soap for the guest bathroom or powder room.

The recipe makes two large shaped soaps when 3" plastic heart ornaments are used for the molds. Prepare the heart molds by conditioning well with a thin layer of petroleum jelly. Place a few red rosebuds into the bottom of the heart molds. Use chopped dried rose petals instead of the rosebuds for a more practical bar.

SOAP RECIPE

Melt together:
1 cup grated strawberry scented transparent soap
1/4 cup water

Add after the soap has melted:
10 drops rose oil

Mix the rose oil in the melted soap. Pour into the mold. Let harden before unmolding. (Because the heart ornament I used is made from hard, rigid plastic, I placed it in the freezer before unmolding.)

To make a three-dimensional heart soap, use a 1/4 cup of melted soap to "glue" the unmolded pieces together. Place the melted, cooled and slightly thickened soap between the two molded hearts and press together. Don't worry if the soap squishes out of the seam--just let it harden, then trim. ❏

50

ROSE SPICE HAND MOLDED SOAP

These are old fashioned soaps with a spicy rose scent. Hand molding is a very easy process that's suitable for children. This recipe makes five to six 2" diameter soap balls.

SOAP RECIPE

Melt together:
1 cup grated soap
1/4 cup rose water
1/4 cup coconut oil

Add after the soap has melted:
1/4 teaspoon cinnamon powder
Red candle dye melted in 1 tablespoon almond oil
10 drops rose oil
5 drops cinnamon oil

After the soap has cooled and thickened, scoop out a small handful of the soap and roll into a neat ball. Repeat until all the soap has been molded. As the soap cures, press into firmer, smoother balls. ❏

SOAP JEWELS

These translucent balls look like semi-precious stones. Since you start with colored and scented glycerine soap, there is no need for many additives. Save some of the grated soap to add after the melting process for an interesting crystalline-like texture.

The recipe can make many soap pebbles in a variety of sizes. Making this soap can be a fun educational project for children learning about different rock formations--green soap can be emeralds, purple soap can be amethysts, dark red can be garnets, and white can be quartz.

SOAP RECIPE

Melt together:
2 cups grated transparent glycerine soap
1/4 cup glycerine
1/4 cup water

Add after the soap has melted:
1/4 cup grated soap of the same color

When the soap has cooled, scoop out small amounts and roll into irregular pebbles of different sizes. As the soap cures, press into firmer, smoother balls. Polish with a bit of petroleum jelly and a soft cloth.

CITRONELLA SOAP

Everyone in the family can benefit from a bar of hand-milled soap--even the family dog! The added citronella and eucalyptus keep fleas and ticks away. It has the added benefit of leaving the dog smelling fresh and clean.

Whipping the soap makes a floating bar that's handy when bathing a squirming dog. (Whipped soap is less attractive, but it does the job.) This recipe makes three bars when whipped or two bars if unwhipped. I used a large, rounded soap mold for this recipe, but any large, deep mold will work.

SOAP RECIPE

Melt together:
1 cup grated castile soap
1/2 cup water

Add after the soap has melted:
10 drops citronella oil
5 drops eucalyptus oil
1 tablespoon dried, crushed pennyroyal leaves

Mix the ingredients into the melted soap. With an electric mixer, whip the soap until it has doubled in volume. Spoon the soap into the prepared molds, pushing it into the molds as best you can. (The beating action cools the mix, so work quickly.) If the mixture has cooled off and thickened so much you can't put it into the molds, hand mold the soap into large balls. ❑

SOAP MOLDED IN A LUFFA

For this soap, slices of luffa sponge are used as the molds for a unique "sponge-soap" bar.

SOAP RECIPE

To prepare the luffa sponge:
Cut the luffa sponge into 2-1/2" slices with a serrated knife. With sharp scissors, remove the inner pieces of the sponge, leaving a tube. (Save these pieces for making the Luffa Scrub Soap). Wrap the luffa with four layers of plastic wrap, pulling the plastic wrap tightly over one end of the tube and securing the plastic wrap close to the edge of the other end of the tube with a thick rubber band (a thin band will cut into the sponge). Trim excess plastic wrap level with the top of the sponge mold. Your sponge is now ready to pour in the soap.

Make soap and mold:
Make soap, using the recipe for Peppermint Refreshment Soap on page 40. Pour the soap into the prepared luffa sponge molds. Let harden. Remove plastic wrap. There is no need to unmold the soaps. ❏

HONEY BEE SOAP

This is a smooth, light fragrance soap. No colors or fragrance oils were added, so it's a very simple recipe. I used a three dimensional beehive candle mold, but you could use any shape you wish and decorate the soap with painting or decoupage.

SOAP RECIPE

Melt in a double boiler and hold over hot water:
1 tablespoon beeswax

Melt in microwave or on top of the stove in a double boiler:
1 cup melted opaque soap base

Add:
1 tablespoon honey

Mix hot, melted soap and melted beeswax. Add the honey and stir until melted. Pour into prepared mold. Unmold when hardened. Let cure on a drying rack. ❏

SNOWFLAKE SOAP

Snowflake Soap is made by adding grated white soap to a clear base. It's pretty when molded in star shapes.

SOAP RECIPE

Here's How:

Grate white soap and transparent soap in separate containers. Don't mix them. Melt the transparent soap base, following the general instructions for "How to Make Hand-Milled Soap." After the transparent base soap has melted, add some grated white soap to the mix just before pouring.

CONFETTI SOAP

Confetti Soap is made by adding slivers of grated colored transparent soap to an opaque white soap base. I like to use the transparent glycerine soaps found in bath product outlets. The round soaps were made using the recipe below. The heart shaped soap was made with red transparent glycerine soap, using the recipe for Snowflake Soap.

SOAP RECIPE

Here's How:
Grate transparent soap and white soap in separate containers. Don't mix them. Melt the white base soap, following the general instructions for "How to Make Hand-Milled Soap." After the white base soap has melted, add the grated transparent soap to the mix just before pouring.

To make color chunk soap, simply cut the transparent soap into chunks with a knife instead of grating. You'll see large pieces of color when you slice the soap. ❏

NOVELTY MOLDED SOAPS

You can mold almost any shape or subject in soap, thanks to the wide selection of candy, plaster, and three dimensional candle molds available. When using molds, you'll get the best results using soap recipes, such as Cinnamon Orange Soap, Milk and Honey Soap, and Rose Spice Soap, that don't include large-piece additives, or by using the microwavable soap bases available at crafts stores.

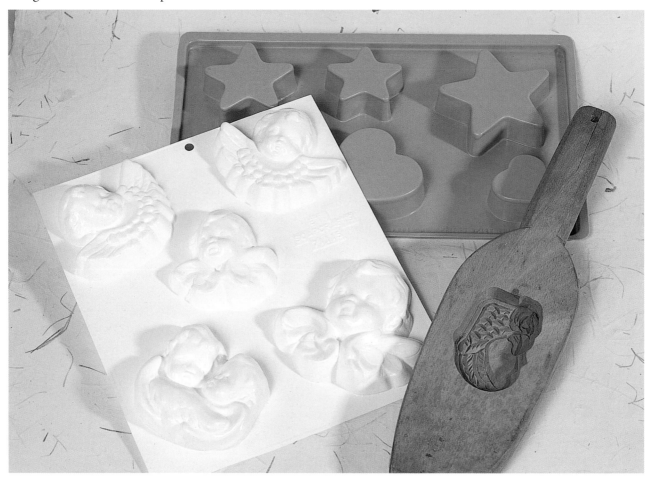

Because microwavable soap bases make a smoother soap than remelted grated soap, they perform better in more detailed molds. The soap I used was a high quality vegetable oil soap enriched with vitamin E oil and coconut oil. Most hand-milled soap recipes make a soap that is a bit thick for small or detailed molds.

Molded soaps.

OCEAN FRESH MOLDED SOAP

These soaps were created with both opaque and transparent microwavable soap bases. The only additives are colorants and fragrances. Candy molds, traditional shell shape molds, and plaster molds are all suitable for crafting these little gems.

General Instructions for Molded Soap

Melt the soap in the microwave or in a double boiler on top of the stove. Do not overheat this soap-- if you do, it could warp your molds. For a cup full of grated shavings, one minute in the microwave, on high, is just long enough to melt the shavings--you should have about 1/2 cup when melted. Add colorants and fragrances just before pouring.

- Always prepare more than you think you will need to fill the mold, so no soap goes to waste. If some is left over, pour in a PVC pipe mold or hand mold into balls.

- For added color and interest, add grated transparent soap to the transparent or opaque soap base. Stir in the grated soap just before pouring. ❏

Suggested Scents:

For sea theme soaps, fresh scents are best. Eucalyptus, rosemary, bayberry, lavender, rain, ocean, and peppermint are suitable. All these fragrances blend well together; combine them to create your personal aromas.

Molded Clear Soaps

To make these transparent soaps, use a transparent glycerine microwavable soap base. Microwavable soap bases are produced especially for home crafters and are easily obtained from craft stores and by mail order. They offer more creative molding opportunities than hand-milled soaps made from a commercial soap base.

Transparent soaps are generally created by melting soap with alcohol instead of water at high temperatures. The added alcohol is a drying ingredient. Because of the high temperature required and the use of alcohol, making transparent soap at home can be dangerous. ❏

DECORATING
SOAPS

Smooth, plain bars of soap can be decorated with paints, decoupaged with motifs, or gilded with luster wax. They can be whimsical or formal and coordinated with colors or themes.

PAINTING SOAPS

Painting is an easy and inexpensive way to quickly add a decorative touch to your soaps. Use smooth, unblemished bars of soap and waterbase paints such as acrylic craft paints. Apply the paint with small brushes or use wooden toothpicks and the dip-and-dot method. Use these soaps for decoration only.

Dip-and-Dot Technique
for Painting Roses

The dip-and-dot technique is an easy way to paint little roses. You'll need red, pink, green, and gold acrylic paints and wooden toothpicks.

1. With a toothpick, place a drop of red paint on the soap and a drop of light pink paint right beside it.
2. With a toothpick, swirl the colors together, creating the rose bloom.
3. To make leaves, place a drop of green paint beside the rose. With a toothpick, pull the drop of paint to a point to create a leaf shape.
4. Create rosebuds by placing a drop of red paint and pulling it to a point like the leaf. Place a green dot at the base for the calyx. Pull the paint with the toothpick to frame the bud with greenery.
5. For added interest, add a series of gold dots with a toothpick. ❑

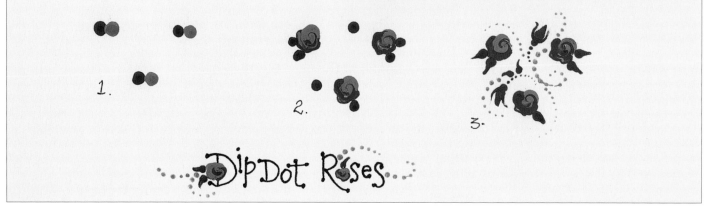

GOLDEN LUSTER SOAP

Soaps can be given a golden luster or a gilded look by rubbing with gold luster wax or by dry brushing with metallic acrylic paint.

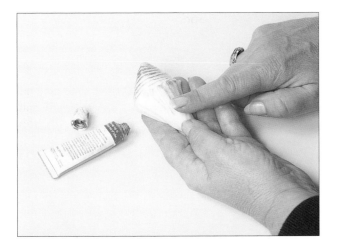

RUBBING WITH WAX

Gold luster wax, used for highlighting furniture and accessories, can also be used to add luster to soaps. Using your finger, simply rub the wax over the surface of the soap. Stop when the amount of gold is to your liking.

DRY BRUSHING WITH PAINT

To dry brush soap, use metallic acrylic paint and a flat artist's paint brush. To highlight the details on molded soap, pick up a very small amount of paint on the brush and wipe the brush over the soap, just touching the raised details. Do not use too much paint-- acrylics are waterbase, and too much paint will start to dissolve the soap. ❏

DECOUPAGED SOAP

Decoupage, the art of adding motifs to a surface, is an easy way to decorate hand-milled soaps or store bought bars. The motifs can come from a variety of sources: paper cutouts, self-adhesive stickers, rub-on transfers, or decals. Choose soap bars with a smooth surface for the best results. Adding a wax coating over the decoupage will make the motif last. When used, the soap will dissolve from the back of the bar and the motifs stays in place.

TECHNIQUES FOR DECOUPAGE

Using paper cutouts:
Glue on paper motifs cut from decoupage paper and wrapping paper with craft glue.

Using self-adhesive stickers:
Simply press self-adhesive stickers in place on the soap.

Using rub-on transfers:
Paint a thin layer of clear water-based varnish on the top of the soap bar. Let dry. Rub on the transfer, following package instructions. (Rub-on transfers will not adhere to the soap without the varnish undercoat.)

Using decals:
Apply to soap, following package instructions.

The Santa is cut from decoupage paper. "Merry Christmas" is a rub-on transfer.

Even designs from napkins can be used as decorative motifs on your decoupaged soap.

ADDING A PROTECTIVE WAX COATING

A wax coating over the motif will protect the motif so it will last the life of the soap. The wax protects one side of the soap as the soap is used from the other side.

1. Place 1" of water in a saucepan or skillet large enough to hold a smaller pan. Place a block of paraffin in a smaller pan and place it in a larger pan. Bring the water to a low boil to melt the wax.
2. When the paraffin wax has completely melted, dip the decoupaged surface of the soap in the wax. **Only dip one side of the soap**--you don't want to seal the whole bar. Dip as many times as needed to get rid of bubbles. Let cool.
3. To polish the waxed surface, rub with a piece of nylon stocking. ❏

The Victorian motifs are stickers. The little garden boy was cut from decoupage paper.

MAKING BATH SALTS

Bath salts are made from an alkaline base that neutralizes the acids on the skin so fragrance clings to the body. The scents are soothing, and the salts are relaxing and healing. Lying in a warm, scented bath not only gets you clean--it's relaxing and refreshing. A fragrant bath by candlelight is a refuge from the stresses of modern life and is a luxury that is affordable to everyone.

Bath salts are made from simple ingredients:

Baking Soda (Sodium Bicarbonate) - Baking soda is a mild alkaline salt used in bath salt formulas offering soothing and softening qualities. It is also a good salt base for absorbing fragrances; when the salts are dissolved in bath water they release the scent.

Citric Acid - Citric acid is a preservative obtained by the fermentation of citrus fruit sugars. It is used with baking soda to create fizzy bath salts. Citric acid is highly astringent and is a great toner for the skin. I found it less expensive when purchased in bulk from a wine supply store rather than at a pharmacy. The citric acid sold in grocery stores for keeping fruit from turning brown didn't fizz well and was the most expensive.

Coarse Salt - Coarse salt is used as the base for fragrant bath salts. I prefer the large, chunky crystals from the health food store for the most attractive salts. The salts neutralize your skin so the fragrant oils cling and make your skin smell beautiful for hours. Salt is also healing and soothing on your skin as you soak in the bath.

Cornstarch - Cornstarch is used in the solid, fizzing Bath Blitz as a filler and binder.

Epsom Salts - Epsom salts are mild alkaline salts that disperse easily in water. They are excellent in bath salt blends for soothing skin inflammations and muscle aches. Use Epsom salts alone with added fragrance oils or mix with other salts to create blends. The fine textured, sparkling grains are attractive in clear bottles.

Sea Salt - Sea salt is an excellent salt base for fragrant bath salts when a fine, granular salt is preferred. You also can use Dead Sea salts (found at health food stores and specialty shops) in salt blends for their curative properties. They are far more expensive than regular sea salt, but make an exotic addition to the Silk Bath.

The salts are the fixative that holds the scents and colors. I have bottles of bath salts I use for display that have kept their scents and colors for years.

The quality of the oils is very important in the bath salt recipes. Essential oils and good quality fragrance oils make superior scented products. Food coloring works well for adding color to bath salts.

A number of recipes for bath salts are included here, as well as the technique for making solid fizzing bath salts. (Every gift basket should include these!)

BASIC BATH SALTS RECIPE

This basic recipe makes six to eight applications.

1 cup Epsom salts
10 to 20 drops fragrance oil

1 cup coarse salt
10 drops food coloring

Place the salts in a large bowl and mix well. Scoop out about 1/2 cup in a small bowl. Add the drops of fragrance oil and food coloring to the salts in the small bowl and mix well. Add the blended mixture to the large bowl a little at a time until you are pleased with the color strength. Pour your salts in a glass jar with a tight fitting lid. Shake every day for one week before packaging.

To Use:

Draw a warm bath and add 1/4 cup of the fragrant salts to the running water. Hop in and relax, inhaling deeply to experience the soothing qualities of aromatherapy. ❏

Sea Salts

These refreshing and energizing salts are pretty colored blue. The eucalyptus oil makes this a nice head-clearing blend when you have a cold.

Making Bath Salts with Children

Bath salts are easy for children to make--and they're always a welcome gift for mothers and grandmothers. This can be an inexpensive project for schools, scouts, and church groups.

Give each child a clean glass jar. Let the child measure the Epsom salts and coarse salt in the jar. Let an adult add each child's choice of fragrance oil and color to the child's jar. Place the lid on the jar and tighten securely. Let the child shake the jar to blend.

Package the salts in cellophane bags, as glass jars can be expensive. Children have fun creating their own labels.

BATH SALT RECIPE

1 cup Epsom salts
1 cup sea salts
10 drops peppermint oil
5 drops eucalyptus oil
5 drops blue food coloring

Follow the general instructions for blending bath salts. ❏

SOOTHING BATH SALTS

Soothing Bath Salts are kind to the skin and the spirit.

BATH SALT RECIPE

To the Basic Bath Salts recipe, add:
1 tablespoon glycerine
10 drops camomile
5 drops ylang-ylang
3 drops clary sage

Other Floral Options:
To the Basic Bath Salts recipe, add your favorite floral scents. Here are some suggested blends:

- Old-Fashioned Garden: 5 drops each of jasmine, honeysuckle and violet

- Victorian Rose: 10 drops rose, 3 drops lavender, 2 drops clove

- Fresh Floral: 10 drops bergamot, 5 drops each of jasmine and rose

SILK MILK BATH

This blend makes your skin silky and smooth. It's a pure delight when you need a luxurious, relaxing soak.

BATH SALT RECIPE

1 cup instant powdered skim milk
1 tablespoon powdered orris root
3/4 cup sea salt (if you can find Dead Sea salts, they are an elegant, exotic addition)

10 drops jasmine oil
7 drops ylang ylang oil
5 drops bergamot oil

Follow the general directions for blending bath salts. ❏

OLD FASHIONED FIZZY BATH SALTS

These salts are left as a powder. The fizzing action happens quickly when they are added to water. Use old-time favorite floral scents like lavender, violet, rose, or honeysuckle. *These salts are not pictured.*

BATH SALTS RECIPE

1 cup baking soda
1/2 cup cornstarch
1/2 cup citric acid
10 to 20 drops fragrance oil
Optional: 10 drops food coloring

Follow the general instructions for blending bath salts. ❏

BATH BLITZ

These solid fizzing bath salts are delightfully invigorating and a literal blast to use in your bath. The solid Bath Blitz acts like a giant effervescent tablet in the bath, creating bubbles and releasing fragrance as it dissolves.

The larger the Bath Blitz form, the longer it lasts. The basic recipe makes six to eight applications or six solid bath forms. *See pages 72-73 for complete recipe and step-by-step instructions.*

Bath Blitz

Here's How

1. Assemble all the ingredients. Place the salts in a large bowl and mix well.

BATH BLITZ RECIPE

Use the Old-Fashioned Fizzy Bath Salts recipe and these step-by-step instructions to create the Bath Blitz. Choose deep molds with large details. There is no need to use petroleum jelly in the molds.

After you master these simple steps, you will be able to produce solid bath salts very quickly.

Additional Supplies You Will Need

- Wax Paper - You will need wax paper for solid fizzing bath salts. They will stick to anything else.
- Water mister: - A mister with a fine spray is needed to make solid fizzing bath salts.
- Thin cardboard - A piece of cardboard is needed for flipping out solid bath salts from the mold. Cardboard is also useful for making templates for cutting soaps into shapes.

2. Scoop out about 1/2 cup in a small bowl. Add the drops of fragrance oil and food coloring to the salts in the small bowl and mix well. Add the blended mixture to the large bowl a little at a time until you are pleased with the color strength.

3. Remove approximately 1/3 cup of the blended, colored salts to a small bowl. Spritz these lightly with a fine mist of water. **Do not over mist,** or your bath salts will start to fizz up! With your hands, so you can judge the dampness, mix the salts well. The salts need to just be damp enough to hold together. If needed, mist again and mix. This is enough for one shape.

TIPS

- If your molded salts break, just remold.
- If your salts seem to "grow" and puff out, you have added too much water! Place the salts in the small bowl and mix in some dry salts to stop the fizzing action. Remold. ❏

4. Pack the damp salts into the mold. Press down hard to pack the salts in, adding more if needed. Pack only one mold at a time.

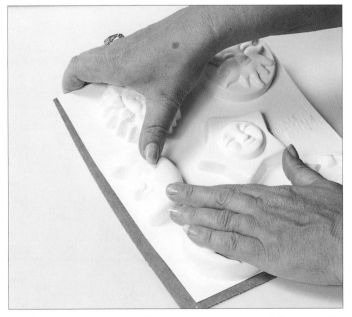

5. Place a piece of thin cardboard over the mold and flip over. The solid bath form will fall out. Be gentle!

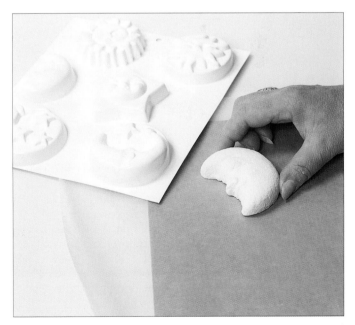

6. Carefully slide the molded salt form on a wax paper covered board or cookie sheet. Let dry overnight.

MAKING
BATH OILS

Bath oils soften your skin with a fine film of oil that scents the air as the fragrance is released into the steamy water. They also help soften hard water and look nice when displayed in the bathroom.

Since homemade bath oils do not contain preservatives, they can become rancid over time. The addition of vitamin E oil, an anti-oxidant, helps bath oils last longer, and vitamin E is good for the skin. Herbs and flowers can be placed in the bottle before pouring in the oil to add a decorative touch, but use only dried items--fresh ones will mold and make your oil rancid.

BASIC BATH OIL BLEND RECIPE

1/2 cup almond oil
1/2 cup castor oil
Oil from 6-8 vitamin E capsules
1 cup *either* safflower oil *or* sunflower oil
20 to 30 drops fragrance oil
Optional: a few slivers of candle dye melted in 1/4 cup almond oil, dried herbs or flowers

Blend all the oils together. Place in a glass container with a tight fitting lid and shake or stir every day for a week. (This helps blend the fragrances and allows you to make adjustments.) Before bottling, add coloring oil and dried herbs or flowers, if desired. Makes 2 cups fragrant bath oil. ❏

BLACKBERRY BLISS FOAMING BATH OIL

FOAMING BATH OIL RECIPE

Combine:

1/2 cup mild formula liquid soap or clear dishwashing detergent
1 tablespoon glycerine
1/2 cup castor oil
1/2 cup almond oil
20 drops fragrance oil

12 drops blackberry oil
6 drops bayberry oil
A few silvers of red and yellow candle dyes and a touch of black candle dye melted in 1 tablespoon almond oil

Mix the ingredients well. They will turn nice and milky, but will soon separate into three layers. The dye, if used, will color only the heavier castor oil layer for an interesting effect. ❏

Cinnamon Orange Bath Oil

BATH OIL RECIPE

To the Basic Bath Oil Blend, add:
20 drops sweet orange oil
10 drops cinnamon oil

Place in the bottle before pouring in oil:
Dried orange slices
Broken cinnamon sticks ❏

CHAMPAGNE BUBBLE BATH

Cherish your quiet time and treat yourself to a warm bath filled with luxurious bubbles! The glycerine and sugar are the secret for big, long lasting bubbles. This mixture is also excellent for blowing big, fragrant bubbles.

BUBBLE BATH RECIPE

Combine:
1 bottle (about 3-1/2 cups) clear, mild dish-washing detergent with added vitamin E.
1/4 cup glycerine
1 Tablespoon sugar
20 - 30 drops fragrant oil
10 drops food colouring

Mix together all ingredients gently until sugar is dissolved. Fragrance for women include rose, jasmine and lavender oils. Children love tangerine or green apple where men prefer spicy, citrus blends.

MAKING MASSAGE OILS

Massage oils, in the form of solid massage bars or liquids, are soothing and nourishing to the skin. Scent them with essential oils for the benefits of aromatherapy. Dried botanicals add decorative touches to bottled liquid massage oils.

SOLID MASSAGE BARS

This wonderful smooth bar melts readily when rubbed into your hands before smoothing on your skin. The main ingredient, cocoa butter, is solid at room temperature but melts at body temperature.

This recipe fills three to four small molds. Use the fragrance blend suggested or create your own. The menthol in the peppermint oil gives the bar a tingly-cooling quality.

MASSAGE BAR RECIPE

Combine:
1/2 cup melted cocoa butter
10 capsules vitamin E oil
1 tablespoon melted coconut oil
10 drops rose oil
8 drops peppermint oil
5 drops ylang-ylang oil

Mix all ingredients. Let cool a bit, then pour into molds and let harden. There is no need to condition the molds before pouring.

MASSAGE OIL BLENDS

This is a light blend that is absorbed into your skin, leaving it soft and silky, not greasy. It's a little more expensive to produce because there really aren't any substitutes for sweet almond oil and essential oils in a massage blend.

Basic Blend Massage Oil	Rose Massage Oil	Lavender Massage Oil
1 cup sweet almond oil	1 cup sweet almond oil	1 cup sweet almond oil
Oil from 6-8 vitamin E oil capsules	Oil from 6-8 vitamin E oil capsules	Oil from 6-8 vitamin E oil capsules
20 drops essential oil, scent of your choice	20 drops rose oil	20 drops lavender oil
Optional: Dried botanicals of your choice	Dried rosebuds	Dried lavender buds ❏

MAKING FACIAL SCRUBS

Facial scrubs, made of soap and dried botanicals, cleanse, stimulate, and soothe the skin. Simple to make and attractive when displayed in a glass jar or in a basket, they're a usable potpourri.

Here's How:

Gently mix the ingredients together in a large bowl. Store in a jar or a basket. *To use:* Place 1/4 cup of the blend in a cotton scrub bag (instructions for making the bags are below). Tie tightly. Wet the bag well, then rub over your face or body with a gentle, circular scrubbing action. Discard contents after use. Rinse the bag with warm water and lay flat to dry.

OATMEAL FACIAL SCRUB RECIPE

The grated soap cleanses and the camomile and oatmeal add a delicious apple-pineapple scent as they relax and soothe your skin. This recipe makes 12 applications.

Combine:

1 cup dried camomile   1 cup regular oatmeal
1 cup grated soap (If you wish, use a beauty bar with added moisturizing cream.)

ROSE MINT SCRUB RECIPE

The grated soap cleanses as the rose petals and mint leaves add fragrance and a cooling, stimulating tonic for your skin. This recipe makes 12 applications.

Combine:

1 cup dried rose petals   1 cup dried mint leaves
1 cup grated soap (If you wish, use a beauty bar with added moisturizing cream.)

SAGE HERB SCRUB RECIPE

The grated soap cleanses as the herbs add their beneficial oils to heal, stimulate, and soothe. This recipe makes 14 applications.

Combine:

1/2 cup dried sage leaves   1/2 cup dried lavender buds
1 cup dried lemon geranium leaves OR lemon verbena
1/2 cup mint leaves
1 cup grated soap (I used a bar of Peppermint-Refreshment Soap.)

COTTON BAGS FOR SCRUBS

I always use herbs in a bag in the bath. Loose, soggy leaves clog the drain, and the last thing I want to do after a relaxing soak is collect all the little pieces left around the tub. Follow these instructions for making your own reusable bags for scrubs.

Supplies to make one bag:

8" x 10" piece of 100% cotton fabric
16" double-faced satin ribbon, 1/4" wide

Instructions:

1. Wash fabric, dry, and iron flat. Fold fabric in half lengthwise, right sides together. (Fig. 1)
2. Fold the ribbon in half and pin in place 5-1/2" from the top on the inside. Arrange the ends of the ribbon so you do not sew them into the seam. (Fig. 2)
3. Pin the rest of the fabric together for sewing. (Fig. 3)
4. Using a small machine stitch, sew the bottom and sides of the bag.
5. Fold the top half of the bag down 2-1/2" to just above the ribbon. Press open the seams and press the fold. (Fig. 4)
6. Turn the bag to the right side and press. Knot the ends of the ribbon to prevent fraying. (Fig. 5) Fill the bag with bath scrub mixture. ❑

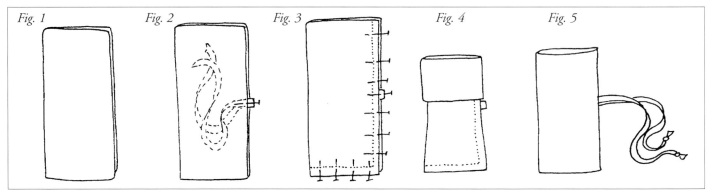

Fig. 1   *Fig. 2*   *Fig. 3*   *Fig. 4*   *Fig. 5*

MAKING BATH TEA BAGS

Bath Tea Bags are blends of dried herbs that add scent and soothing qualities to your bath. Unlike the facial scrubs, they don't contain soap. The bags are meant to be disposable, so choose an inexpensive fabric.

Supplies for one tea bag:
7" x 10-1/2" cheesecloth or cotton gauze fabric
1/4 cup bath herbs
12" thin cord or cotton string
Large-eye needle

Instructions:
1. Fold the fabric in half lengthwise, right sides together. Sew down one long side to form a tube. (Fig. 1)
2. Turn the tube right side out. Move the seam to the center and press flat. (Fig. 2)
3. Mark the center with a pin and sew 1/2" away from the center on both sides. (Fig. 3)
4. Place the bath herbs in both sides of the tea bag and fold up so open ends are together. (Fig. 4)
5. Fold ends and pin. (Fig. 5)
6. Thread the needle with the thin cord or string and stitch the top folds, holding it all together. Remove the needle and tie string in a bow. (Fig. 6) ❏

LAVENDER CITRUS BATH TEA BAGS

Pictured on opposite page

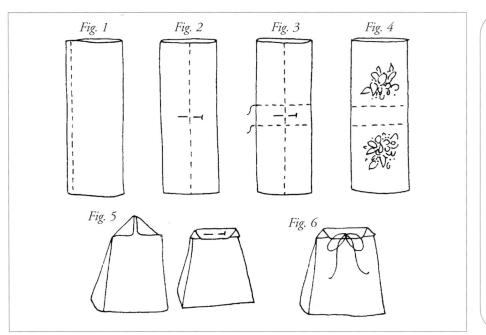

Fig. 1   Fig. 2   Fig. 3   Fig. 4

Fig. 5   Fig. 6

TEA BAG RECIPE

This recipe fills 10 to 12 bath tea bags.

Combine in a bowl:
1 cup dried lavender buds
1 cup dried lemon verbena leaves
1 cup dried orange peel, chopped fine

To use: Simmer one bath tea bag in a pan on top of the stove in one quart of water for 10 minutes to make a fragrant "tea". Pour the tea and the bag into your bath water and relax. Use the wet tea bag to scrub and stimulate your skin. Discard after use. ❏

PACKAGING

When you have taken the time to make beautiful gift soaps and bath products, presenting them in an attractive and fun way is equally important.

SEALING BOTTLES

Bottled oils, bubble bath, and bath salts can be easily sealed with sealing wax. Sealing wax contains a rubber compound which makes the wax act more like a plastic than a wax, so the seal is leak-proof and attractive. (Paraffin and beeswax seals eventually leak--the oils eat right through them.) Dipping once or twice seals the bottle. Natural and white sealing wax can be colored with powdered pigments or candle dyes.

Here's How:
1. Place sealing wax in a shallow foil container. Place the foil container in a saucepan or skillet of water to make a double boiler. The wax melts at 300 degrees F. Watch that the water does not boil over into the wax.
2. Fill the bottle and insert the cork snugly, leaving enough cork sticking out of the bottle to grasp for removal.
3. Wrap cord or ribbon around the neck of the bottle. Twist at the back and keep taut (Fig. 1), then drape over the top of the bottle. Tape in place. (Fig. 2)
4. Invert the bottle and dip into the melted sealing wax, submerging the neck of bottle about 1/2" from the top until an adequate seal has been made. Lift the bottle straight up, letting the excess wax drip away. Let cool.
5. Check the seal to be sure it works. Remove tape. Trim the ribbon.
To open a wax-sealed bottle: Pull the ribbon upwards to break the seal. If any wax residue remains, remove by running under hot water before taking out the cork.

WRAPPING SOAPS

Soaps can be wrapped in plastic wrap, cellophane, or wax paper and packaged in envelopes, boxes, and bags made of paper, cardboard, and cloth. Decorative labels can be made quickly and easily by hand and with a photocopier from colored, handmade, and recycled papers and embellished with wax seals, buttons, rubber stamps, stickers, and calligraphy. Individual Gift Collections will give patterns and specific information on some handmade boxes for your gifts.

DECORATIVE WAX SEALS

Use inexpensive rubber stamps and melted sealing wax to make decorative wax seals for soaps and bottles. The process does not damage the rubber stamp--it can still be used for stamping.

Here's How:
1. Melt the sealing wax in a double boiler.
2. Using a kitchen spoon, spoon out a pool of wax about the size of a quarter on a piece of aluminum foil.
3. Immediately press a rubber stamp in the wax. Let cool a few seconds before removing stamp.
4. Let wax cool completely, then peel away the foil. (If you're not pleased with the result, remelt and try again.)
5. *Optional:* Rub with gold metallic wax to accent.
6. Use thick craft glue to adhere seals to bottles, packages, and envelopes. ❏

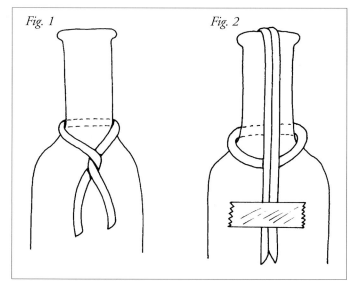

Fig. 1   Fig. 2

Fly away flea soap

Savons Lavender Citrus

Soap Banana

PEBBLES

Chamomile-Oatmeal Soap

Cinnamon Orange

For You

MILK & HONEY

Honey Almond

MAKING LABELS

Making labels is the satisfying finishing step for your wrapped and packaged soaps and bath products. Professional-looking printed labels--in black and white and full color--can be made easily using a photocopier or computer printer on a variety of beautiful papers. Cut them to size and shape with scissors or a craft knife. Or cut labels from card stock, cardboard, or cloth or use buttons, copper plant markers, or die-cut gift tags.

Write the names of products on labels and embellish them with felt-tipped markers or paint pens, which are available in gold, silver, and white from art supply and stationery stores. Labels also can be decorated with calligraphy, stenciling, rubber stamps, and embossing. You can also paint a decorative label on a container with acrylic paints. Secure labels to products with glue, tape, cord, or wire.

You'll find examples galore in the "Gift Collections" section. Labels you can photocopy and reproduce on your choice of papers are printed on the pages that follow.

87

GIFT COLLECTIONS

The products you can make from the recipes in this book can be packaged and combined for beautiful baskets and boxes that make treasured gifts. To create a gift collection, choose a theme that fits the person or the occasion, then use your imagination and the ideas from the following pages to create a unique and memorable offering.

Here are some tips for putting it all together:
- Choose a container that fits the theme. It's especially nice when the container is a gift in itself--a basket, a dish, or a flower pot, for example, that can be used again.
- To display your products attractively, fill the container with a packing material that will hold the products in place and keep them from slipping down. Examples of decorative fillers are excelsior, shredded paper, confetti, and tissue paper. If the container is large or deep, pack it with crumpled newspaper first, then place the decorative filler on top of the newspaper. Include dried rose petals, lavender buds, silk flowers, and preserved leaves to add color. Arrange your wrapped and packaged products on the filler.
- To hold everything together, wrap with cellophane or heavy plastic wrap.

With cellophane:
Use cellophane pieces four times as long as the container is high. For example, if your container and products measure 10" high, cut two pieces of cellophane, each 40" long, from a 24" wide roll. Place them in a cross formation with the container in the middle. Bring up the ends of the cellophane, two at a time, and gather in your hands. Secure with a twist tie. Trim the ends of the cellophane and add a bow and a gift tag to finish.

With plastic wrap:
Plastic wrap is especially effective if you are mailing the gift. Wrap the collection with plastic wrap, pulling the ends of the wrap to the bottom of the container. Secure with tape. You can further "shrink" the wrap and remove wrinkles by heating with a blow dryer. Use heavy plastic wrap for best results. If you have access to shrink-wrapping equipment, use it.

Carpet Fresh

Sea Salts

Cinnamon Orange Bath Oil

Lavender Massage Oil

SAGE HERB SCRUB

SILK MILK BATH

Facial Scrub
Chamomile Oatmeal

KING Co

Floral Bath Salts

89

ROMANTIC ROSE BOWL

An elegant white china cutwork bowl is filled with luxurious treats for bath and body. Lacy looking parchment seals and gauzy rice paper wrappings are feminine and charming. Rose petals make a nest for special soaps in a china bowl and decorate bottles of massage oil and bath oil. The bubble bath is colored a rosy red, and there's a copper wire bubble wand. Handpainted roses adorn the bottles, a small soap, and a scented candle. What a lovely gift for a bride!

The Contents

ROMANTIC ROSE BOWL
The Presentation

Packaging:

- Pour Baby Rose Oil and Rose Bubbles in clear glass bottles. Decorate bottles with wreaths of dip-dot roses painted with acrylic enamel paints. (See "Decorating Soaps," for painting instructions.) Seal with gold trimmed ribbon and white sealing wax.
- Paint Heart-Shaped Molded Soap with roses (see "Decorating Soaps"). Place in a small china bowl with excelsior, rose petals, and Rose Spice Hand Molded Soaps. Wrap with plastic wrap. Tie with gold-trimmed sheer white ribbon.
- Place Heavenly Bath Angels Bath Blitz in cellophane bags with rose petals. Tie bags with ribbon.
- Wrap Heart-Shaped Massage Bar in sheer rice paper. Tie with a ribbon bow.
- Pour Rose Massage Oil in a clear class bottle. Seal with gold wax. Decorate with a gold wax seal and gold-trimmed ribbon.

The Labels: Photocopy the labels on parchment paper. Use a white paint pen to letter and highlight.

The Container: The container is a cutwork white china bowl filled with shredded white tissue.

Nice Additions:

- A bubble wand was made by twisting 19 gauge copper wire into a heart shape. Glass beads were threaded on the handle.
- A painted votive candle wrapped in sheer rice paper. The dip-dot roses on the candle were painted with acrylic enamel paints. ❏

ROSE BUBBLES BATH RECIPE

The glycerine and sugar are the secret for big, long lasting bubbles in your bath. (This mixture is also excellent for blowing big, fragrant bubbles.)

3-1/2 cups clear, mild dishwashing soap or detergent
Oil from 5-6 capsules vitamin E oil
1/4 cup glycerine
1 tablespoon sugar
20-30 drops rose fragrance oil
10 drops red food coloring

Mix all ingredients gently until sugar is dissolved.

HEAVENLY BATH ANGELS RECIPE

To the Old Fashioned Fizzy Bath Salts recipe, page 71, add:
10 drops rose oil
8 drops vanilla oil
4 drops ylang ylang oil

Follow the instructions for making Solid Fizzing Bath Salts, pages 72 and 73. Use a deep cherub soap mold.

BABY ROSE OIL RECIPE

1 cup baby oil
20 drops rose oil
Miniature dried roses

Combine oil and fragrance. Add miniature dried roses. Place in a clear glass bottle.

EGYPTIAN QUEEN BEAUTY BOX

Fit for the queen of any house, this box's theme is carried out with a sophisticated black and gold color scheme, a soap and a box in shape of a pyramid, and stenciled Egyptian motifs.

Sumptuous gold seals and pieces of real gold leaf adorn a bottle of jasmine and bergamot scented bath oil. It's a sure way to give a special person the royal treatment.

The Contents

Golden Jasmine Bath Oil, instructions follow.
Milk and Honey Soap, see "Hand-Milled Soap Recipes."
Silk Milk Bath, see "Making Bath Salts."
Relaxing Eye Mask, instructions follow.
Do Not Disturb Door Sign, instructions follow.

Egyptian Queen Beauty Box

The Presentation

Packaging:
- Pour Golden Jasmine Bath Oil in a glass bottle. Seal with gold sealing wax and gold cord. Add a stamped seal.
- Package Silk Milk Bath Salts in cellophane bags. Decorate with gold seals. Place in collapsible boxes (instructions follow).
- Package Milk and Honey Pyramid Soap in a pyramid box (instructions follow).
- Stencil the door sign, eye mask label, and wooden box with Egyptian motifs.

Labels and Packages: Labels and packages are made from black rice paper and gold printed wrapping paper fused together with spray adhesive. Lettering is done with a gold paint pen.

The Container: The container is a shallow wooden box. The outside is painted with gold paint and decorated with Egyptian motifs stenciled in black. The inside of the box is painted with black paint. Purchase precut stencils or cut your own from Egyptian designs. The plastic fillers are black and gold.

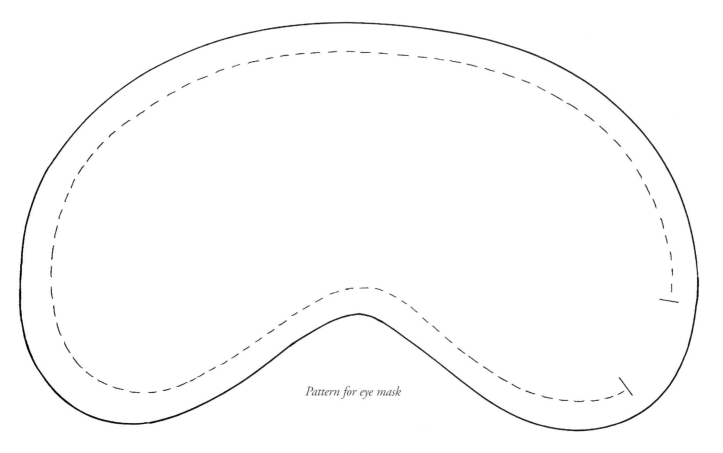

Pattern for eye mask

GOLDEN JASMINE BATH OIL RECIPE

To the Basic Bath Oil Blend on page 74, add:
20 drops jasmine oil
10 drops bergamot oil
1 sheet gold leaf (Composite gold leaf is fine, it need not be 24k!)

Blend oils and add fragrance. Tear sheet of gold leaf into pieces. Place in the bottle before pouring in the oil. (Packages of gilding gold leaf are available at art supply and crafts stores.)

RELAXING EYE MASK

This bag is designed to fit comfortably over your eyes when you lie down to relax. The lavender offers a fresh, soothing scent. Keep the bag in the freezer in a plastic bag so it is always ready to use.

Supplies to make one bag:
9" x 10" piece of satin or soft cotton fabric (A silky Egyptian cotton would be nice.)
1/4 cup flax seed
1 tablespoon dried lavender buds

Instructions
1. Trace pattern on a piece of tissue paper. Pin on fabric and cut out 2 pieces.
2. Place the pieces with right sides together and pin to hold.
3. Sew around the mask, using a 1/2" seam. Leave a small opening for filling.
4. Using a small funnel, pour the flax seeds and lavender buds into the bag.
5. Hand stitch the opening closed using small stitches.

COLLAPSIBLE BOX

Supplies for one box:
8" x 12" piece of rice paper
8" x 12" piece of gift wrap
10" x 3/4" strip of decorative
  paper
Embossing stylus, craft knife,
  ruler
Thick craft glue, spray adhesive

Instructions

1. Fuse the two decorative papers together, wrong sides together, with spray adhesive.
2. Using a craft knife and ruler, cut out a 2" square at each corner to make the box shape. (Fig. 1)
3. With the stylus, emboss all the dotted lines for easy folding. (Fig. 1)
4. Fold and crease along embossed lines. Unfold and lay paper flat.
5. With the inside of the box down, fold A flaps to form points. (Fig. 2) Glue points in place.
6. Pinch the B corners and fold under the A points. (Fig. 3) Glue in place. You now have a box.
7. With your fingers, push in the sides and collapse the box along the creased lines. (Fig. 4) Press the box flat. (Fig. 5)
8. Make a looped band with the decorative paper and glue ends together. Slip the band over the box to hold it closed.

To open: Slip off the band and unfold the box to reveal the contents.

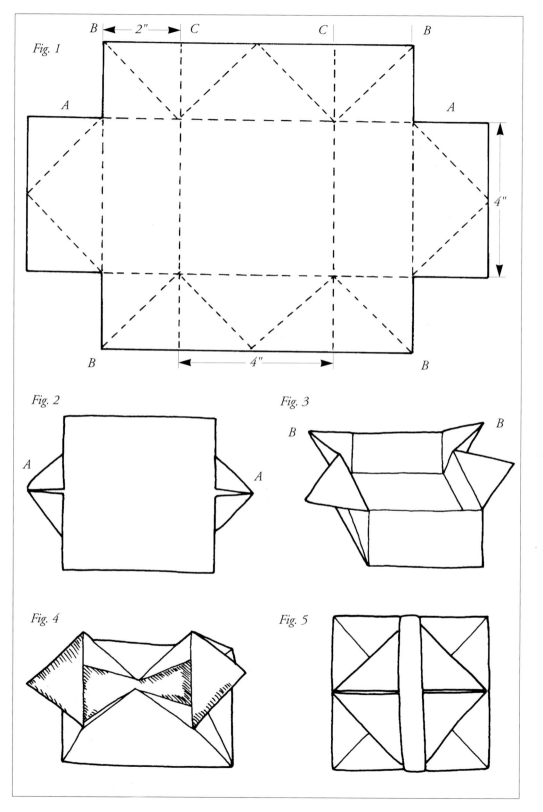

Fig. 1

Fig. 2

Fig. 3

Fig. 4

Fig. 5

PYRAMID BOX

Supplies for one box:
8" x 8" piece decorative paper (hand-made paper or gift wrap)
8" x 8" piece card stock
10" thin gold cord
Embossing stylus, ruler, scissors, 1/8" hole punch
Spray adhesive

Instructions
1. Spray card stock lightly with adhesive. Place decorative paper over card stock. Press together to fuse.
2. Enlarge pattern @143% on a photocopier. (Fig. 1) Cut out. Place pattern on decorative paper and cut out along solid lines.
3. Emboss on dotted lines and fold.
4. Punch a hole in each corner.
5. Place soap in box. Thread cord through holes and tie to secure.

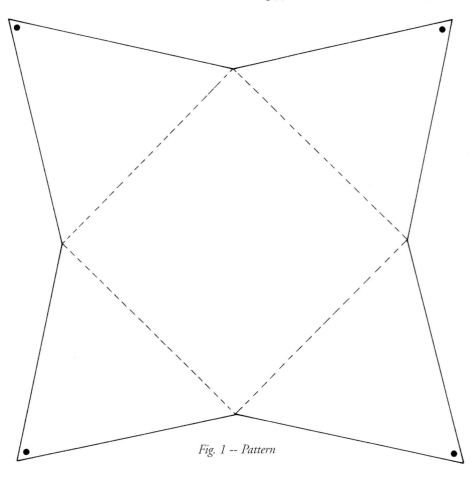

Fig. 1 -- Pattern

DOOR SIGN

Supplies for one sign:
5" x 11" piece decorative paper
5" x 11" piece card stock
Scissors, craft knife, ruler
Gold paint pen
Egyptian motif stencil. stencil brush, gold acrylic paint

Instructions
1. Spray card stock lightly with spray adhesive. Place decorative paper over adhesive. Press together to fuse.
2. Photocopy the half-pattern given. Fold photocopy on dotted line and cut out for full-size. Tape to fused paper and cut out.
3. With a craft knife, cut out space for doorknob.
4. Stencil motif with gold paint. Let dry. Add outlines and lettering (Do Not Disturb - The Queen Is Relaxing) with gold paint pen. ❑

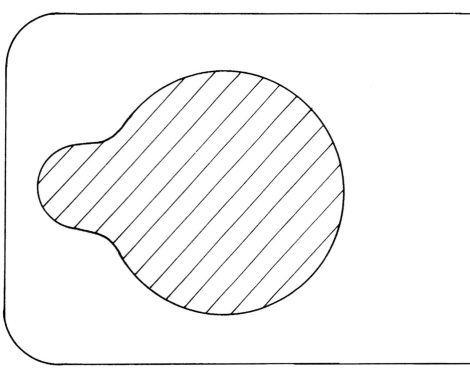

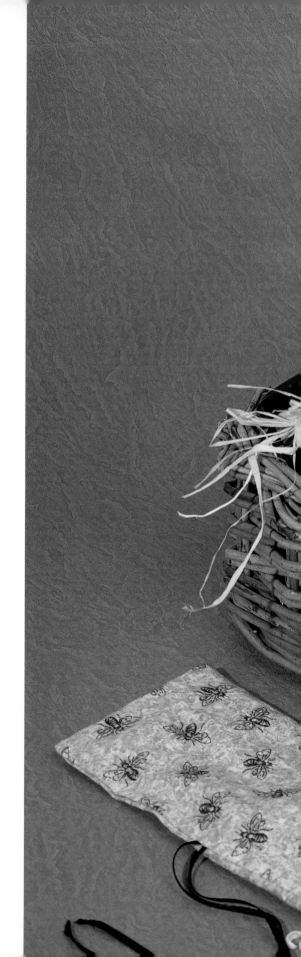

FLOWER GARDEN BASKET

A basket of garden delights awaits the recipient of this collection. The fragrant scents of flowers and honey are sure to attract bees, so a bee motif was used to stamp the labels and the ribbon for the bow, and a bee-patterned fabric was used for the scrub bags. Copper garden plant markers are embossed and used as tags.

The Contents

FLOWER GARDEN BASKET

The Presentation

Packaging:
- Wrap Honey and Almond Soap with tan tissue paper.
- Make seed packet envelopes for Floral Bath Salts from recycled paper (instructions follow). Tie envelopes together with natural raffia and label with a copper tag.
- Place Rose Mint Facial Scrub in a clear glass bottle. Tie natural raffia around the neck of the bottle.
- Make Scrub Bags from bee patterned cotton fabric.
- Pour Blackberry Bliss Foaming Bath Oil in a clear glass bottle. Seal with green sealing wax.
- Mold Honey Bee Soap in a beehive candle mold and wrap in plastic wrap.

Paper Labels: Cut paper labels from tan recycled paper in various shapes to fit jars, lids, and soaps. Included is a pattern for a honeycomb shape to use for labels. Stamp with purchased rubber stamps and black stamping ink (I used a bee stamp) and accent with yellow and orange markers and felt-tipped pens.

Copper Tags: The copper tags on the basket handle and bath salts are copper garden plant markers. Pressure embossed lettering is done with a ball point pen. Sponge lightly with green acrylic paint for an antique look.

The Container:
A natural willow or wicker basket is the perfect container. Fill with excelsior or straw. Tie a bow on the handle with sheer ribbon. (The bee stamp used on the labels can also be used to stamp the sheer ribbon for the bow.) Attach a copper plant marker to the handle as a gift tag.

Nice Additions:
- Hand rolled beeswax candles wrapped with corrugated cardboard and accented with a honey bee
- Fresh, dried, or artificial flowers
- A small straw beehive

ROSE MINT FACIAL SCRUB

See page 80 for facial scrub instructions and recipes.

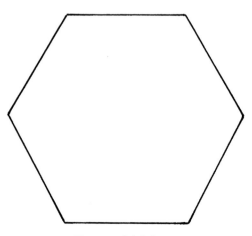

Honeycomb label pattern

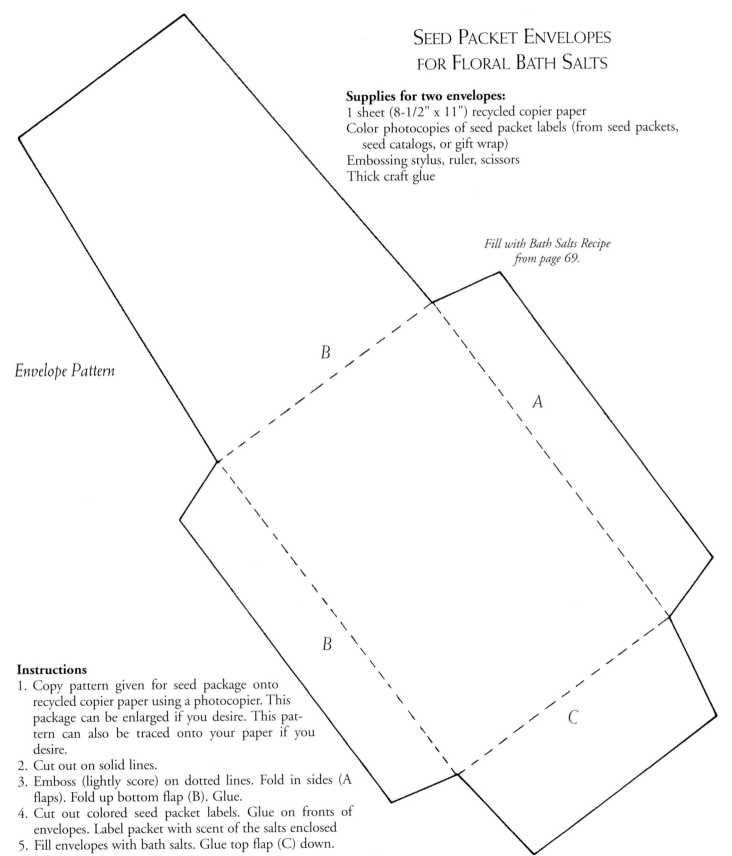

SEED PACKET ENVELOPES
FOR FLORAL BATH SALTS

Supplies for two envelopes:
1 sheet (8-1/2" x 11") recycled copier paper
Color photocopies of seed packet labels (from seed packets,
    seed catalogs, or gift wrap)
Embossing stylus, ruler, scissors
Thick craft glue

*Fill with Bath Salts Recipe
from page 69.*

Envelope Pattern

B

B

A

C

Instructions
1. Copy pattern given for seed package onto recycled copier paper using a photocopier. This package can be enlarged if you desire. This pattern can also be traced onto your paper if you desire.
2. Cut out on solid lines.
3. Emboss (lightly score) on dotted lines. Fold in sides (A flaps). Fold up bottom flap (B). Glue.
4. Cut out colored seed packet labels. Glue on fronts of envelopes. Label packet with scent of the salts enclosed
5. Fill envelopes with bath salts. Glue top flap (C) down.

OCEAN BREEZE CRATE

Refreshing and bracing as a sea breeze, this treasure trove of treats has a nautical theme. Soaps and bath products in the colors of the sea and the sand are presented and decorated with sea shells--you can almost hear the ocean! The distressed-finish wooden crate might have survived a shipwreck and washed up on shore.

The Contents

OCEAN BREEZE CRATE

The Presentation

Packaging:

- Place Ocean Fresh Molded Soaps on a large scallop shell with some excelsior. The shell doubles as a soap dish.
- Mold Peppermint Refreshment Soap in pieces of luffa sponge. Stack and tie with natural raffia.
- Place a bar of Peppermint Refreshment Soap on a wooden soap holder. Tie with a piece of natural color net-like trim.
- Bottle Sea Salts in clear glass and use a sea shell cork. The chevron design in the salts is produced by pouring blue-tinted salts and white salts in layers, then pushing a wooden craft stick down against the inside of the bottle. Make the shell cork by placing a screw through the top of the cork, leaving 1/2" sticking up. Glue the opening of the shell over the screw with thick craft glue. (Using a screw prevents the shell from popping off when the cork is pulled.) Wrap the cork and the top of the bottle with raffia.

Labels: Photocopy labels on natural parchment copy paper. Letter with a black felt-tip pen.

The Container: A wooden crate was painted with a distressed wood paint kit to give it a sun-bleached, weathered look. Drill holes in the ends, loop pieces of rope through the holes, and knot rope inside to make handles. Fill crate with excelsior.

Nice Additions:

- A natural cotton wash cloth, rolled and tied with natural raffia and a spray of eucalyptus (This one is hand knitted and provides gentle exfoliation for washing. I found the instructions on the label of a skein of unbleached cotton yarn. These wash cloths can also be crocheted.)
- A wood and natural bristle nail brush in the shape of a seashell. ❏

OCEAN BREEZE LABELS

PEPPERMINT REFRESHMENT SOAP

See chapter on "Hand-Milled Soap Recipes" for instructions and recipes for this and other hand-milled soaps.

TROPICAL RAINFOREST SET

The vibrant colors of the tropics and the lush scents of mango, banana, coconut, and mint adorn a selection of soaps. Bath salts are molded to make blue Butterfly Bath Blitz. Festive, colorful tree frogs, built from plastic clay and painted in bright colors with acrylic paints, perch on a bottle of tropical fruit-filled bath oil and the natural birch wood container. Natural wood buttons and raffia keep things labeled and organized.

The Contents

TROPICAL RAINFOREST SET

The Presentation

Packaging:
- Wrap Banana Slice Soaps individually with brightly colored tissue paper. Stack and tie with raffia.
- Wrap Mango Mint Shampoo Bars with brightly colored tissue paper.
- Pour Stimulating Bath Oil in a clear glass bottle. Seal with gold wax. Add a toy frog or make your own plastic clay frog for decoration. (see below)
- Package Butterfly Bath Blitz in clear cellophane bags with purple confetti.
- Wrap Confetti Soap in plastic wrap.

Wooden Tags: The wooden tags are natural wood buttons, 1-1/4" to 1-1/2" in diameter. Natural raffia was looped through the holes to hold them in place. Lettering was done with a gold paint pen.

Frogs: The frogs were hand built from plastic clay right on the bath oil bottle and the birch wood container, then baked according to directions on the package. Paint with acrylic enamel paints (bright green, bright yellow, bright red). Finish with a clear gloss varnish. Glue to crate and bottle. If using a toy frog simply glue to bottle.

The Container: A round birch wood container is decorated with a climbing frog and filled with purple confetti. Use preserved magnolia leaves for accents.

BUTTERFLY BATH BLITZ RECIPE

To the Bath Blitz recipe on page 71, add:
10 drops mango oil
10 drops lime oil
Blue food coloring

Add the fragrance oils and coloring to the Bath Blitz recipe. Use a butterfly soap mold.

STIMULATING BATH OIL RECIPE

To the Basic Bath Oil Blend recipe in previous chapter "Making Bath Oil" add:

15 drops bergamot oil
10 drops peppermint oil
5 drops each lavender and sweet orange oils

Mix oils. Pour in bottle with dried pineapple pieces, dried papaya pieces, and dried mint leaves.

Prehistoric Bowl

A reconstructed clay pot stenciled with cave painting motifs holds a cache of treasures to delight kids of all ages. Amber soap is molded with plastic bug surprises. A stenciled cloth bag holds prehistoric pebbles--Soap Jewels that resemble gemstones. Sage scents an herbal scrub and a Fragrant Fire Bundle.

The Contents

Sage Herb Scrub, see "Making Facial Scrubs."

Stenciled scrub bags, see "making Facial Scrubs." These scrub bags were made with unbleached cotton and stenciled with cave art designs.

Amber Soap, see "Hand-Milled Soap Recipes."

Soap Jewels, see "Hand-Milled Soap Recipes."

Fragrant Fire Bundle, instructions follow. ❏

The Presentation

Packaging:
- Place Sage Herb Scrub in a cellophane bag and tie with raffia.
- Place Soap Jewels in a stenciled cloth bag.
- Wrap Amber Soap with clear plastic wrap.
- For Fragrant Fire Bundle, cut pieces of fresh sage about 5" long. Tie bundle with natural raffia. Place on a drying rack for about a week to allow the fresh sage to naturally dry. Throw these into an evening fire and let the aroma soothe you.

Labels: Cut labels from different colors of green paper in leaf shapes, using decorative scissors. Punch with a hole punch or awl and tie on with narrow black ribbon or natural raffia.

Gift Tag: Stencil a cave art design on a scrap of unbleached cotton. Cut out shape and fray edges. Cut out a card from green paper to fit the stenciled scrap. Glue scrap on card.

The Container: The container is a clay flower pot that was broken, then glued back together with the pieces a bit askew. The pot was sponged with earth tone acrylic paints, stenciled with cave art designs, and finished with a coat of waterbase varnish. ❏

SAGE
HERB
SCRUB

AMBER
SOAP

PEBBLES

ANTIQUE SPA BOX

Old-fashioned scents of lavender, lemon verbena, and citrus waft from a decoupaged, antiqued tea box. Blue glass bottles with sumptuous green and gold seals and sheer ribbons hold fizzy bath salts and lavender-scented massage oil.

The Contents

Violet Fizzy Bath Salts, see "Making Bath Salts." Use basic recipe and scent with violet fragrance oil.

Lavender Massage Oil, see "Making Massage Oil." Use basic Massage Oil recipe and scent with lavender essential oil. Add dried lavender buds and dried orange peel to bottle.

Lavender Citrus Soap (3 bars), see "Hand-Milled Soap Recipes."

Lavender Citrus Bath Tea Bags (4 bags), see "Making Bath Tea Bags." ❏

ANTIQUE SPA BOX

The Presentation

Packaging:
- Wrap Lavender Citrus Soap in gold tissue paper. Wrap with ribbon and accent with a gold wax seal.
- Make Lavender Citrus Bath Tea Bags with purple gauze fabric. Stitch the bags closed with metallic gold thread.
- Place Violet Fizzy Bath Salts and Lavender Massage Oil in cobalt blue glass bottles. Seal with gold wax. Accent with gold wax seals. Tie lengths of sheer green ribbon around the necks of the bottles.

Labels: The labels are photocopied on parchment copy paper and antiqued with tea. (Soak a tea bag in hot water for five minutes. Use the tea bag like a sponge to pat the labels. Let dry.) Use a gold paint pen to accent. Letter names with a black pen.

The Container: The container is a cardboard tea box, decoupaged with torn pieces of brown paper grocery bag. (You could also use a cigar box.) Complete instructions follow. Line with printed tissue and dried lavender buds.

DECOUPAGED TEA BOX

Supplies to make one box:
Recycled cardboard tea box
Plain brown paper, torn into 2" pieces
Decoupage finish
1" foam brush
Burnt umber acrylic paint
Acrylic extender painting medium
Small natural sponge
Old toothbrush
Gold paint pen
1 yd. green sheer ribbon
Small brass charm

Instructions:
1. Brush decoupage finish on one side of a brown paper piece. Place on box. Smooth out any bubbles or wrinkles with your fingers. Continue with remaining pieces, overlapping them to cover box completely, inside and out. Let dry.
2. Brush two coats of decoupage finish over the entire box, inside and out. Let dry between coats. Let dry.
3. Mix extender and burnt umber paint. Sponge box with paint mixture for an antique look. Let dry.
4. Thin paint mixture with water. Spatter box, using an old toothbrush. Let dry.
5. With the gold paint pen, letter the names of the herbal ingredients in script (Lavender, Lemon Verbena, Citrus Peel).
6. Glue ribbon and brass charm on front of box. Wrap ribbon around box and tie end in a bow. Glue in place.
7. Glue a label on the outside that lists the contents. Glue a label on the inside with instructions for using the bath tea bags. ❏

LABEL PATTERNS

DAISY FRESH POT

Pick a bouquet of daisies to accompany this flower pot filled with a fresh-as-a-daisy collection fragrant with the clean scent of camomile. Parchment envelopes and wax paper are used for the simple see-through packages.

The Contents

Camomile Oatmeal Soap, see "Hand-Milled Soap Recipes."
Soothing Bath Salts, see "Making Bath Salts."
Camomile Oatmeal Facial Scrub, see "Making Facial Scrub."
Cotton Scrub Bags, see "Making Facial Scrub." (These scrub bags were made from a natural cotton waffle weave dish cloth and tied with ivory satin ribbon.)
Camomile Blossom Bath Oil, see "Making Bath Oil."

The Presentation

Packaging:
- Pour Camomile Blossom Oil in a clear glass bottle. Trim with white rick rack. Seal with white wax.
- Place Soothing Bath Salts in a parchment bag (instructions follow). Accent with white rick rack and a silk daisy.
- Top a round of Camomile Oatmeal Soap with a silk daisy. Wrap with wax paper. Place label over ends of paper.
- Package Camomile Oatmeal Facial Scrub in a parchment envelope (instructions follow).

Labels: Photocopy labels on white paper. Color the daisy centers with a yellow felt-tipped pen. Letter with a black felt-tipped pen.

The Container: The container is a ceramic flower pot. Fill with excelsior. Add a bouquet of fresh daisies.

CAMOMILE BLOSSOM BATH OIL RECIPE

To the Basic Bath Oil Blend on page 74, add:
15 drops camomile oil
10 drops lavender oil
5 drops each of rose oil and sage oil

Mix oils and fragrance oils. Place 1/8 cup dried camomile blossoms in bottle and pour in oil.

Pattern for Parchment Envelope

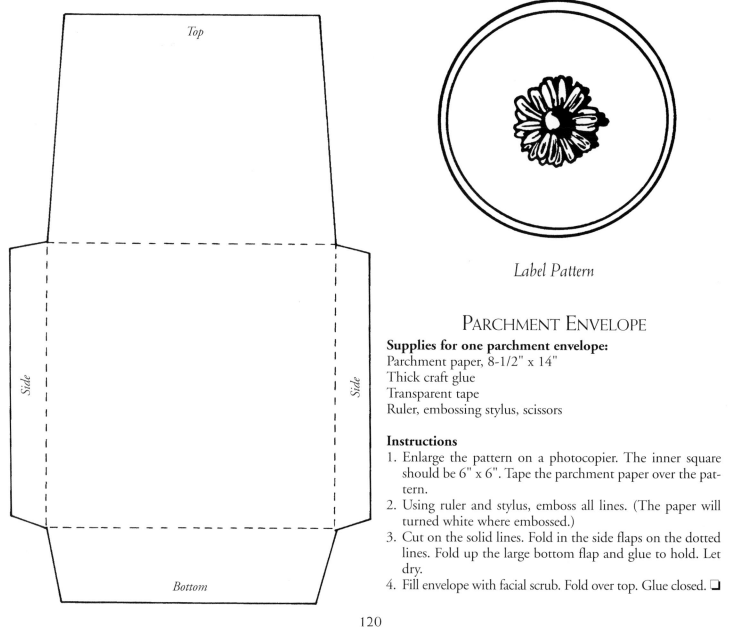

Top

Side

Side

Bottom

Label Pattern

PARCHMENT ENVELOPE

Supplies for one parchment envelope:
Parchment paper, 8-1/2" x 14"
Thick craft glue
Transparent tape
Ruler, embossing stylus, scissors

Instructions
1. Enlarge the pattern on a photocopier. The inner square should be 6" x 6". Tape the parchment paper over the pattern.
2. Using ruler and stylus, emboss all lines. (The paper will turned white where embossed.)
3. Cut on the solid lines. Fold in the side flaps on the dotted lines. Fold up the large bottom flap and glue to hold. Let dry.
4. Fill envelope with facial scrub. Fold over top. Glue closed. ❏

Parchment Bag

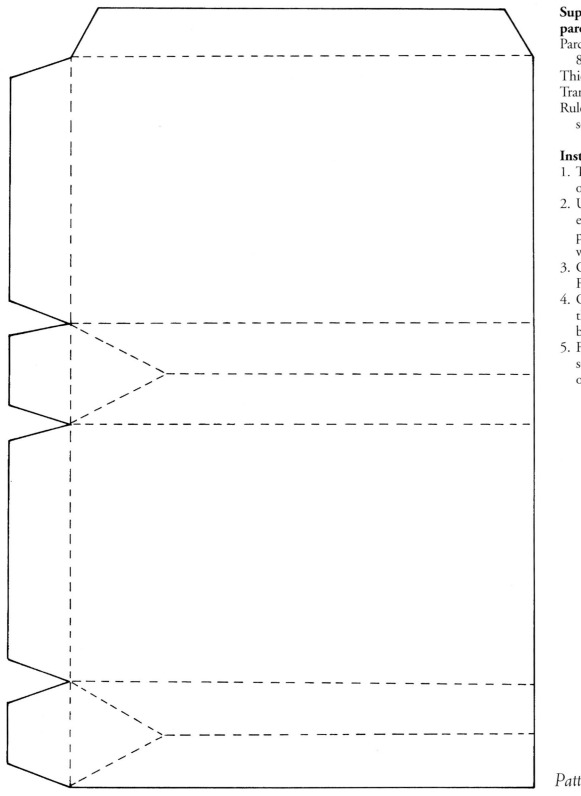

Supplies for one parchment bag:
Parchment paper, 5-3/4" x 8-3/4"
Thick craft glue
Transparent tape
Ruler, embossing stylus, scissors, stapler

Instructions
1. Tape the parchment paper over the pattern.
2. Using ruler and stylus, emboss all lines. (The paper will turn white where embossed.)
3. Cut on the solid lines. Fold on the dotted lines.
4. Glue the bottom flaps and the side flaps to form the bag. Let dry.
5. Fill bag with 1/4 cup scented bath salts. Fold over top. Staple closed.

Pattern for Parchment Bag

DOGGY BOWL

Here's a trio of canine can't-do-withouts to keep your favorite Fido comfortable, clean, and flea-free--all thoughtfully contained in a stainless steel water bowl.

The Presentation

Packaging:
- Package Carpet Deodorizer in an aluminum storage tin.
- Place Fly Away Flea Soap with some excelsior in a cellophane bag. Tie with black twill tape.

Labels: Photocopied labels on white paper. Letter with a red felt-tipped pen.

The Container: The container is a new stainless steel water dish.

The Contents

Doggy Comfort Bag, instructions follow.
Carpet Deodorizer, instructions follow.
Fly Away Flea Soap, made from the Citronella Soap recipe, see "Hand-Milled Soap Recipes."

122

CARPET DEODORIZER RECIPE

Make this fragrant mixture to place in your vacuum cleaner bag. When you vacuum, you will fill the house with fragrance. The botanicals also repel flies and ticks, deodorize the carpet, deter moths, and take away pet smells. Use 1/2 cup for each application. Replace when you change the bag. This recipe makes three cups (six applications). Place 1/2 cup in your vacuum bag.

1 cup vermiculite
1/2 cup dried camomile
1/2 cup dried lavender buds
1/2 cup dried mint leaves

1/2 cup dried eucalyptus leaves
10 drops citronella oil
10 drops peppermint oil

Mix citronella and peppermint oils with vermiculite. Combine with dried botanicals. ❏

DOGGY COMFORT BAG RECIPE

This comfort bag is excellent for older dogs with arthritis or for a dog recovering from surgery who needs a warm, comfortable rest. The herbs help to repel fleas and ticks. To heat, place the bag in microwave for 1-1/2 minutes on high. The bag will stay warm for about one hour.

Supplies for one bag with cover:
1 red bandanna (22" x 22")
3 cups flax seeds
1/4 cup **each** dried camomile, lavender buds, and dried mint leaves

Instructions
For the washable cover:
1. Fold the bandanna, right sides together, so two ends overlap by 2" in the center. (Fig. 1)
2. Measure in 10" and cut. Set aside cut piece.
3. Sew around the outside of the bag. Press seams open and turn to the right side.

For the pillow:
1. From the remaining piece of the bandanna, cut out two pieces, each 9" x 9".
2. Pin with right sides together, and sew around edges using a 1/2" seam. Leave a small opening.
3. Press open seams. Turn right side out.
4. Pour in the seeds and the botanicals. Sew the opening, using small stitches. Slip the filled bag into cover to finish your pillow.

Fig. 1

CINNAMON ORANGE BOX

Spicy and citrus fragrances scent the soaps and bath oil in this attractive heart-shaped box. Colorful Citrus Slice Soaps are whimsical and fun.

The Contents

The Presentation

Packaging:
- Arrange Citrus Slice Soaps on a piece of corrugated cardboard. Wrap with cellophane. Tie with natural raffia.
- Pour Cinnamon Orange Bath Oil in a clear bottle. Seal with copper sealing wax.
- Package Cinnamon Orange Soap in corrugated cardboard pouches. (See instructions that follow.)

Tags: Cut from recycled cardboard. Punch holes with a hole punch. Lettering was done with a black felt-tipped marker. Accent individual items with dried orange slices, cinnamon sticks, natural raffia, and wired paper cord.

The Container: The container is a heart-shaped natural papier mache box covered with woven paper ribbon. Gift tag is recycled cardboard. Decorate with dried orange slices, dried botanicals, and cinnamon sticks. Tie with natural raffia.

CORRUGATED CARDBOARD POUCH

Supplies
8" x 9" piece of thin corrugated cardboard
3" x 4" piece clear cellophane
Embossing stylus, ruler, craft knife, scissors, thick craft glue

Instructions
1. Enlarge pouch pattern on a photocopier. Cut out pattern.
2. Tape pattern to the smooth side of the corrugated cardboard. Emboss on the dotted lines. Cut on the solid lines.
3. With craft knife, cut out window. Glue cellophane over window on smooth side.
4. Fold pouch and glue side flap in place. ❏

Pattern for Pouch

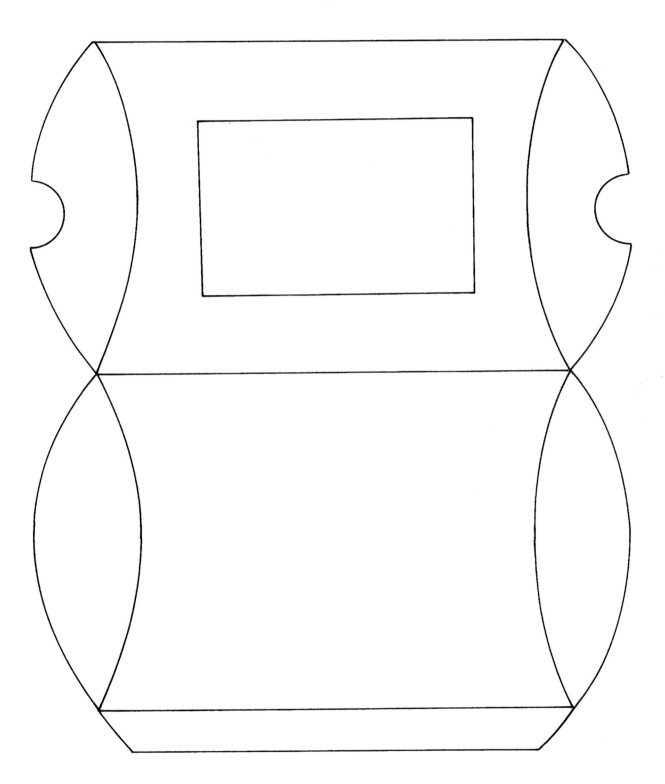

INDEX